STUPID MOVIES LINES

THE STUPIDEST THINGS EVER UTTERED ON THE SILVER SCREEN

ROSS & KATHRYN PETRAS

D0784783

Michael O'Mara Humour

ABOUT THE AUTHORS

Ross and Kathryn Petras, siblings and media junkies, are the authors of the best-selling *The Stupidest Things Ever Said*, *The Nastiest Things Ever Said*, *The One Hundred Stupidest Things Ever Done*, *Stupid Sex* and a number of other books. They live in the New York area.

First published in Great Britain in 2000 by
Michael O'Mara Books Limited
9 Lion Yard
Tremadoc Road
London SW4 7NQ

www.mombooks.com

First published in United States in 1999 by Villard Books, Random House

A CIP catalogue record for this book is available from the British Library

ISBN 1-85479-497-3

1 3 5 7 9 10 8 6 4 2

Designed and typeset by Keystroke, Jacaranda Lodge, Wolverhampton

Printed and bound in Great Britain by Cox & Wyman, Reading, Berks

INTRODUCTION

Bad movie lines have a way of repeating on you, like heartburn. These are the weird, odd, bizarre or stupid bits of dialogue that make the movies you are watching simply terrible, unwatchable except in a wonderfully perverse way. Sometimes, of course, the movie itself is good, but a bad line insinuates itself, and long after the movie is over, there is that lingering aftertaste – much like a rancid french fry in an otherwise wonderful meal.

This book is our labour of love for cinematic heartburn.

It celebrates the movie lines that have stayed with us long after our VCR was shut off: the lines that made us laugh when we were supposed to be crying; the ones that made us shake our heads; the ones that amazed us with their breathtaking inanity; and others that, in some ineffably enjoyable way, nauseated us.

We've collected approximately four hundred of the lines that we think are the best of the worst – hundreds of non sequiturs, cloyingly awful romantic lines, terrible jokes, moronic monologues, failed comebacks, awful dialogue. It's a grab bag of lines that in a more perfect world would have ended up on the cutting room floor – but fortunately were saved for us to . . . savour.

Our reasoning for this somewhat different form of film preservation is simple. Just as the American Film Institute labours to preserve classic films so future generations can enjoy them, we have a similarly lofty goal: to preserve classic stupidity as uttered on the silver screen.

Stupid movie lines are well-deserving of this attention. In any cinematic year, there are many dull lines, many blah lines, many lines that are merely so-so. But there are very few lines in the thousands of screenplays written and produced that are so

3

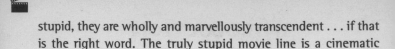

stupid, they are wholly and marvellously transcendent . . . if that is the right word. The truly stupid movie line is a cinematic treasure of sorts, and should be so treated.

So, to be sure that the public recognizes the inverse artistry of these lines, we've watched hundreds of films, from big-budget disasters to grade Z horror to failed existential art house productions. Aided by the efforts of legions of stupid-movie-line fans from around the world who shared their favourites with us and friends and family, we have collected what we feel are the cream of the stupidest movie lines in history for all of us to enjoy.

One note for aficionados of very bad cinema: we have focused on stupid movie lines alone. But there are others – in the past and present – who have made it their mission to share with the public an appreciation of bad movies in general. We heartily recommend the works of the following people: among others, Golden Turkey Award founders Harry and Michael Medved, Michael Sauter, Edward Margulies and Stephen Rebellow, the Phantom of the Movies, and the dozens of intrepid souls who have taken bad movies into cyberspace on such websites as Ohthehumanity.com, badmovies.org, razzies.com (website of the annual Razzie awards), and stinkers.com.

Picking bad movie lines is obviously a subjective thing, so if you find that we have omitted some of your favourite lines, please don't hesitate to contact us. We're already putting together a sequel and would love to have your input. Let us know if you wish to be credited in print underneath your quotation. We can be e-mailed at **stupidest@aol.com**, or reached at our website that celebrates all areas of stupidity: **stupidest.com**. Or you can write to us care of the publisher.

On Absolutely Clever Movie Ads in 1966:

The Big Comedy of Nineteen-Sexty-Sex!

Ad for *Boeing Boeing*, 1966

On Acidic Living Rooms, Alive and Pulsating:

John (Bruce Dern), as an LSD 'guide' to Paul (Peter Fonda): You want to go over the bridge back into the living room, right?
Paul (Peter Fonda), who is tripping: The living room. The LIVING room!

The Trip, 1967

On Admissions, Astounding:

Christopher, I've just thrown a head of cabbage at a cat!

Vincent Price as the nervous husband whose first wife's spirit has returned in a cat's body in *The Tomb of Ligeia*, 1965

On Advice, Bad Girl Style:

Just remember, men can see much better than they can think. A low-cut neckline does more for a girl's future than the entire Britannica encyclopaedia!

Bad girl Betty Anderson (Terry Moore) modelling a new frock in *Peyton Place*, 1957

On Alcoholics, Priestly Pep Talks for:

Father Conroy: You think you're going to find what you lost in that bottle?
Phil (drinking again): Maybe in the next one. I haven't tried all the bottles yet. But maybe I should get the Christmas spirit. Isn't this the time of year when all the little girls and boys suddenly start to behave?
Father Conroy: That's not the real secret of Christmas, Phil. Give it a try! Stop bending your elbow and start bending your knee!

The drunkard Phil (Ray Walston) and the reforming Father Conroy (Bing Crosby) in *Say One for Me*, 1959

On American Honeybees, Our Friends the:

The African killer bee portrayed in this film bears absolutely no relationship to the industrious, hard-working American honeybee to which we are indebted for pollinating vital crops that feed our nation.

Title card at the end of *The Swarm*, 1978

On Anthropologists, Asexual:

Will you stop calling me a lady? I'm not a lady, I'm an anthropologist!

> Tanya, an American anthropologist in the Indonesian jungle, as she is stripping down to her black bikini in *Lady Terminator*, 1988 (Indonesia)

On Ape-Date Problems:

Come on, Kong, forget about me! This thing's just never going to work, can't you see?

> Jessica Lange as Dwan, explaining to the lovesick Kong why she can't be his girlfriend, in *King Kong*, 1976

On Ape-Men, Unbearable Conversations with:

Jane: I'm Jane Parker. Understand? Jane. [pointing to herself] Jane.
Tarzan (touching her): Jane . . . Jane . . . .Jane.
Jane: Yes, Jane. [pointing to him] You? [no answer – pointing to herself] Jane.
Tarzan (touching her): Jane.
Jane (pointing to him): And you? You?
Tarzan (thumping chest): Tarzan. Tarzan.
Jane: Tarzan.
Tarzan: Jane. Tarzan. Jane. Tarzan. Jane. Tarzan. Jane. Tarzan. Jane. Tarzan. Jane. Tarzan. Jane –
Jane: Oh, please stop! Let me go! I can't bear this!

> *Tarzan, the Ape Man*, 1932, with Maureen O'Sullivan and Johnny Weissmuller

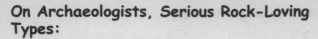

On Archaeologists, Serious Rock-Loving Types:

Mrs Stewart: Everything's a big joke with you, except your damn rocks!
Dr Stewart: You're right. I never joke about my rocks.

Conversation between archaeologist (Tim Ryan) and his wife (Joan Severance) about a large rock he is working on in *Runestone*, 1990

On Arguments, Getting the Last Word in:

Her: I have a life of my own – you didn't create me!
Him: As a matter of fact, I did. I sewed you together out of corpses. And I can uncreate you, too.

Jennifer Beals and mad scientist Sting having an argument, before his hate turns to lust in *The Bride*, 1985

On the Atomic Age, Great Moments in:

These days they blame the atom for everything. Bad health, bad crops, bad weather. Now it's grasshoppers.

Soldier talking about the giant grasshoppers that have begun appearing in *Beginning of the End*, 1957

B

On Bad Girls, Knowledgeable:

Good girl: If you get a high school diploma, then you can earn things for yourself.
Bad girl: With what I've got, I don't need a diploma.

Youth Aflame, 1959

On Bad Girls, 1950s Style:

Mother: Cigarettes, beer, all grown up!
Marjorie: We might as well face it: I've gone to the dogs.

Natalie Wood as the growing ingénue in the title role in *Marjorie Morningstar,* 1958

On Beatniks, Why They Give Small Parties:

And there aren't very many real people left. The only real people I know are dead. Pushed into nuthouses... lobotomy ... junk ... suicide ... or really cooling it and saying nothing to nobody.

Beatnik girl in smoky jazz club in *Once a Thief,* 1965

On Becoming a Man, the Cold Truth About:

Farmer: You left your boyhood behind you.
Parrish: Yes, one night under the ice at the North Pole
. . . It separated the men from the boys.

Troy Donahue in the title role, back from the Navy, in *Parrish*,
1961

On Becoming a Vampire, Why It's Not Cool:

Aw, man, you're jivin' me! Look, man, I don't mind bein'
a vampire and shit, but this really ain't hip!

Newly bitten young man, now a vampire, to Blacula in the
blaxploitation film *Scream, Blacula, Scream!*, 1973

On Being a Citizen of the British
Commonwealth, Benefits of:

You can't mesmerize me. I'm British!

Peter Cushing making the monster understand what's what
in *At the Earth's Core*, 1976

On Being English, Benefits of:

Inspector: What if one of you is the monster?
Peter Cushing: We're English!

Horror Express, 1976

THE MOST CLOYING STUPID MOVIE LINES EVER WRITTEN

Take a lisping toddler, a wide-eyed kid, or clean-cut teen, throw in some cutesy problems with the English language, some theoretically adorable mixed metaphor or some ostensibly charming naïveté, and you have one of the quintessential types of the stupidest – and possibly most nauseating – movie lines ever written.

These are celluloid moments designed to evoke a sentimental tear or smile, but instead evoke the insatiable urge to retch.

On Compliments, Nauseating:

Oh, goshers, Lady Buddy! Every time you're coming here you're looking more prettier!

> Dondi (David Kory), the poor little Italian orphan, to 'Patti Page, the Singing Rage' in *Dondi*, 1961

On Martians, Cutesy Children's Reception of:

Billy: Who are you?
Kimar: We're from Mars. Don't be afraid, we have children just like you on Mars.
Betty: What are those funny things sticking out of your head?
Kimar: Those are our antennae.
Betty: Are you a television set?

> Earth children meet the Martians in *Santa Claus Conquers the Martians*, 1964

On Biblical Dialogue That Fortunately Never Made the Bible:

Jesus: What is your name, my friend?

James the Younger: James. Little James. They call me 'little' because I'm the youngest. What is your name?

Jesus: Jesus.

James: Ah, that's a good name!

Jesus: *Thank you.*

The Greatest Story Ever Told, 1965

On Big-Vocabulary Words, Helpful Movie Definitions of:

His cells are growing at an accelerated – or speeded-up – rate.

Doctor explaining what's happening in *The Amazing Colossal Man*, 1957

On Big-Vocabulary Words, More Helpful Movie Definitions of:

You're describing schizophrenia, aren't you? I knew there was something wrong with me. I had no idea it was – insanity!

Joan Crawford coming to a big realization in *Possessed*, 1947

On Birthdays, What Not to Do on:

It's my birthday and I don't want to go to a mental hospital!

Distraught heroine (Crystal Bernard) complaining to her mother in *Slumber Party Massacre II*, 1987

On Breasts, Giving Up on:

Oh, to hell with 'em! Let 'em droop!

Jennifer (Sharon Tate) giving up her bust improvement exercises in *Valley of the Dolls*, 1967

On Bummers, Big:

Ever since Karen got killed it's been a real drag.

Teen party boy in *The Horror of Party Beach*, 1964

On Bystanders, Snappy Questions from:

You mean, they were *murdered*?

Bystander to a cop, after seeing headless victims of the rampaging giant sea creature in *The Monster of Piedras Blancas*, 1958

C

On Caesarian Lines, Chilled:

They Came . . . They Thawed . . . They Conquered . . .

Ad line for *The Chilling*, 1989

On Canine Distinctions, Essential:

Daughter: She has real wolves.
Mum: I don't want you touching those animals. They're not like . . . dogs.

Daughter (Rumer Willis) having a conversation with Mum (Demi Moore) about a not-very-favourite aunt in *Striptease*, 1996

On Capitalists, Deep Dreams of:

Corporation man: I want to do one small good thing before I die.
Wife: Such as wallowing in that tramp?

Corporate-guy-turned-freak Kirk Douglas and wife (Deborah Kerr), discussing his relationship with mistress Faye Dunaway in *The Arrangement*, 1969

On Catchphrases, Corny:

Well, shuck my corn!

Sadie (Louise Fazenda), a denizen of Hillbillyland, in *Swing Your Lady*, 1938

On Catchphrases, Ones That Thankfully Didn't Catch on:

Slurp my butt!

Hudson Hawk (Bruce Willis) telling the boys from the Mob to get lost in *Hudson Hawk*, 1991

On Christopher Columbus, Sleazy:

She's a fine vessel. Perhaps a bit top-heavy and too narrow of beam. [turning to his mistress and leering] Not unlike someone else I know!

Georges Corraface in the super-bomb *Christopher Columbus: The Discovery*, 1992, starring Tom Selleck as King Ferdinand

On Civilization, Good Points About:

Professor Konrad: Perhaps this is a civilization that exists without sex.
Lt. Larry Turner: You call that civilization?
Professor Konrad: Frankly, no.

Paul Birch and Patrick Waltz, *Queen of Outer Space*, 1958

THE STUPIDEST MOVIE MONOLOGUE

A stupid monologue is a masterpiece in stupid movie writing. Instead of relying on interplay between two characters, the writer of the stupid monologue must rely on the dramatic build-up . . . or lack thereof. Often what the monologue lacks in eloquent words, it makes up for in overwrought acting – making this a truly memorable film moment.

When done successfully (which is to say, badly), these are monologues that far from achieving the level of Hamlet's 'To be or not to be' instead sink happily into a mire of overwritten muck and over-the-top hysteria. The cream of the crop go it one better by throwing in repetition, improvisation, and the requisite screaming of four-letter words.

The following, the closing scene and supposed psychological climax of the film *Tracks*, meets these criteria. A wild-eyed Dennis Hopper, who is at the cemetery after escorting his dead Vietnam War buddy's body cross-country by train, reaches the pinnacle (which is to say, the nadir) of stupid movie monologues.

I love . . . I love . . . I love . . . I really love, I really do love, I really do love. I *love*, I *love*, I *LOVE* and I *hate* and I *hate* and I *hate* and *HATE*, and because I love, 'cause I love, I HATE 'cause I love, I HATE, 'CAUSE I LOVE, 'CAUSE I LOVE – YOU MOTHERF***ERS! YOU MOTHERF***ERS! . . . T.C.B., take care of business, T.C.B., take care of business . . . Okay, okay, all right. Let's cool it out here, you didn't just be in the army for nothin', mister. They send you to Nam, don't they? They send you there. You don't want to go to Nam. You *don't* wanna go to Nam. I'll take you to Nam. I'll TAKE YOU TO NAM. You *WANNA* go to Nam? You *WANNA* go to Nam? *YOU WANNA GO THERE?*

I'LL TAKE YOU THERE! I'LL . . . [pause] You don't wanna go to Nam, you don't wanna go to Nam, I'll take you to Nam, I'll take you to Nam. YOU WANT TO GO TO NAM? *YOU WANT TO GO TO NAM?*

> Dennis Hopper as a Vietnam vet at the gravesite of his friend, yelling his lines as he jumps into the grave, opens the coffin, pulls a helmet, rifles and ammo out of the coffin, then emerges – helmet on and two rifles in hand – as the frame freezes and credits roll, in *Tracks*, 1976

On the Classics, Unclassy:

Porthos: If you can name me one thing that is more sublime than the feel of a plump pink nipple between my lips, I'll build you a new cathedral.
Aramis: Forgiveness.
Porthos: Forgiveness? [faaaaarrrt] Forgive me?

> Gérard Depardieu (Porthos) and Jeremy Irons (Aramis) establishing their characters at the beginning of *The Man in the Iron Mask*, 1998

On Come-ons, Limp:

Man: You have a very soft body.
Woman: Soft? I work out two hours a day to keep it firm!
Man: You have very soft skin over a very firm body.

> Young man trying to seduce Loni Anderson in *Three on a Date*, 1978

On Come-ons, Slick:

If you ever decide to swim the Channel, I'd like to handle the grease job!

Bad guy Tony (Robert Wagner) ogling Holly (Debbie Reynolds), before he becomes a good guy in *Say One for Me*, 1959

On Come-ons, Terrible:

You don't look like my ex-wife at all. She was well-bred and rather frail, except for her famous mammalia. You look more like a cow than my late wife. Oh, no offence. I'm very fond of cows. Moooooo!

Robert Mitchum to Liz Taylor in *Secret Ceremony*, 1968

On Comedic Moments, Flat Not Phat:

Emma, Victoria, Melanie C., Melanie B., Geri. You've been charged with releasing a single that was no more kicking than your previous ones. Nor does it have such a phat bass line. You are sentenced to having your next record enter the charts at 171 and having it fall out completely the following week.

Judge (Stephen Fry) sentencing the girls in *Spice World*, 1997

On Coply Wisdom:

After a psychologist says a murderer's note doesn't make sense:
That's because we don't understand it yet.

Cop to psychologist in *Knight Moves*, 1992

On Cops, Great Moments in Forensic Deduction and:

One thing's sure. Inspector Clay's dead. Murdered. . . . And somebody's responsible!

> Police officer making an amazing discovery and deduction in *Plan 9 from Outer Space*, 1959

On Cops, Not So Bright:

I'll have to see him before I believe he's invisible.

> Policeman who doesn't quite know what to believe in *The Invisible Man Returns*, 1940

On Cops, Philosophical Statements from:

You may know about corpses, fella, but you've got a lot to learn about women.

> Policeman to morgue worker in *Autopsy*, 1978

On Cops, Serial Killer Identification and:

I tell you what it is, Fanducci. It's a big guy in a bulletproof dog suit. I know a serial killer when I see one.

> Top cop Chief Richardson (Lawrence Tierney) to his detective, about a mysterious killer who rips his victims' faces off and who is immune to gunfire in *Runestone*, 1990

On Cops, Viewpoints About Genius Aliens and:

He makes me feel like a moron – but I like him.

> Police chief (Kenneth Edwards) discussing the Venusian who
> has come to Earth to save us from our nuclear sins in *Stranger
> from Venus*, 1954, starring Patricia Neal

On Cops, Wisdom from:

The minute the doctor falls in love with the patient, he's
about as useful as a papoose.

> Policeman (Thomas Mitchell) to the psychiatrist (Lew Ayres),
> who's falling in love with one of his twin patients in *The Dark
> Mirror*, 1946

On Co-stars, Helpful Defining Moments of:

Captain: Well, the magnetic field on the dark side could
exert a gravitational pull, and, uh . . .
Co-pilot: And that means that this is a natural
decompression chamber, doesn't it, sir?

> The captain (Sonny Tufts) forgetting his line and being helped
> by his co-star, Douglas Fowley, in *Cat Women of the Moon*,
> 1954

On Courtroom Defences, Great Moments in:

It's not a crime to be a great lay.

> Willem Dafoe defending Madonna to the district attorney in
> *Body of Evidence*, 1993

On Cute Female Assistants, Typically Dumb 1960s Variety:

Female assistant: What makes you think they're in that
   time co-ord . . . co-ord . . .
Male scientist: Coordinate!

   Smart scientist in the time-travel laboratory helping his not-
   so-smart female assistant with that tough word 'coordinate'
   in *Journey to the Center of Time*, 1967

On Cuteness, Excessive:

Boys, boys! Calm down! Haven't you heard of the word
   'compromisation'?

   Ginger Spice (Geri Halliwell), being cute, in *Spice World*,
   1997

On Cutting Off Male Organs, Key Points About:

Surgeon: You realize that once we cut it off, it won't grow
   back. I mean, it isn't like hair or fingernails or toenails
   or nothing.
Myron: What do you think I am, some kind of idiot? I
   know that!

   John Carradine as the surgeon to Rex Reed as Myron, just before
   Myron's sex-change operation in *Myra Breckinridge*, 1970

D

On Daddies, Dubious:

Molly: Daddy, she says I bounce when I walk. Do I? Do I?
Daddy: Heh, heh, heh. In a pleasant and unobjectionable
way.

Sandra Dee as Molly and Richard Egan as Daddy discussing
Molly's repressive mother in *A Summer Place*, 1959

On Daddies, Dubious Drinking and Pill-Popping:

Then he drives around with her in that van of his, drinking,
taking pills – I'm sure he doesn't *think* about putting a
seat belt on her.

Stripper Erin Grant (Demi Moore) worrying about her
daughter's safety with her ex in *Striptease*, 1996

On Dames, Space Driving and:

Maybe space driving is easier for dizzy dames. There's less
traffic in outer space.

Narrator in Italian import *Sexy Proibitissimo*, 1963

On Dancers, Fishy:

You look good. You move like a rainbow trout.

Television producer (Phil Harris) to a dancer who is auditioning in *The Cool Ones*, 1967

On Darkness, Dreadfully Descriptive:

It's as dark as the inside of a cow's third stomach.

Description of a dangerous cave in *What Waits Below*, 1985

On Dates, Bad:

Boy: She got lost in the pyramids. The mummy will have her for supper!
Girl: Oh, the poor kid!

Boy reporting his girlfriend is lost in the Mexican hinterlands in *Wrestling Women vs. the Aztec* [sic] *Mummy*, 1964

On Daughters, a Little Weird:

Gee, I hope nobody thinks we're father and daughter. I hope they think you're a dirty old man and I'm your broad.

Deborah Raffin as the daughter to father Kirk Douglas, who is picking her up at the airport in *Once Is Not Enough*, 1975

On the Dead Burying the Dead:

Promise me, Brad. If we die, you won't bury me here.

Upset actress to actor in *Demon Wind*, 1990

THE STUPIDEST ROMANTIC SCENES

A man, a woman, a sunset, and soft music welling up on the soundtrack. This is the stuff of romance on the silver screen.

But all too often, at the very moment that the hero is gazing into the heroine's eyes, her lips are trembling with desire, and the lush strings are reaching a crescendo – he opens his mouth and says his lines . . . and it's bye-bye love, hello hysteria.

Sometimes it's a matter of a little too much – too much emoting, too much sighing, too much sticky sentiment. Other times, it's a bizarre non sequitur or a completely inappropriate response. Still other times, it's the juxtaposition of ostensible romantic dialogue just as a giant plastic leech is ravaging the countryside – something we suspect happens less often than depicted on screen – that makes the love scene ludicrous.

However, whatever the reason for the inadvertent thud where tender emotion was intended, these moments of ridiculous romance are certainly provocative . . . and always entertaining.

On Touching Moments, Literal:

Mickey Rourke: I had a father for a while. When he disappeared, I barely spoke for years. I stayed in the third grade a long time.

Carré Otis (unbuttoning her blouse): Just reach out and touch me.

Mickey Rourke, as a Harley-riding billionaire, and Carré Otis as his sensitive attorney in *Wild Orchid*, 1990

On Romance, Slimy:

When I'm sitting here with you, I don't even think about slime people . . .

Hero to heroine in *The Slime People*, 1962

On Love Scenes, Annoying:

Sergeant Brett: You're the sweetest poison that ever got into a man's blood! I love you! I *want* you! . . . Listen, you little wildcat, you're the only real thing that's ever happened to me. And nobody, nothing could ever make me let you go.

Louvette the half-breed: I love you so terrible bad, I feel good. . . . My heart sings like a bird!

Robert Preston and Paulette Goddard in *North West Mounted Police*, 1940

On the Dead, Deadness of:

The dead look so terribly dead when they're dead.

Earnest young hero Tyrone Power in *The Razor's Edge*, 1946

On the Dead, Moving Problems of:

I know he's returned from the dead, but do you really think he's moved back in?

Detective questioning psychic about the undead sicko they're trying to deal with in *The First Power*, 1990

On Dead, Partly and Completely:

Maybe I didn't kill him completely dead.

Willie (Brian Wimmer), the 'normal' brother, after he and his subnormal sibling accidentally wound someone during a botched kidnapping in *Late for Dinner*, 1991

On Dialogue That Fortunately Never Made the Bible:

Aw, she's lyin'. They're Christians. Arrest 'em.

Roman soldier in Roman marketplace in *The Sign of the Cross*, 1932

On Diplomacy, Great Moments in:

Army officer: You're doing *what*? Are you mad? You mean you want us to conduct peace negotiations with BUGS?
Scientist: Either that or you can consider praying!

John Saxon in *The Bees*, 1978

On Dirty Old Men, Snappy Comments from:

You girls a bunch of nudists or are you just short of clothes?

Dirty old man to go-go chicks in *Faster, Pussycat! Kill! Kill!*, 1966

On Disembodied Heads, Conversational Openers for:

I'm just a head out here. What are you in there?

> Bodiless head, sitting on a table, to mysterious voice coming from a closet in *The Brain That Wouldn't Die*, 1962

On DJs, Ones We'd Rather Not Hear, Thank You:

Men have destroyed the roads of wonder and their cities squat like black toads; in the orchards of life, nothing is clean or real as a girl, naked to love or be a man with.

> Clint Eastwood as a cool-talkin' DJ in *Play Misty for Me*, 1971

On Doctors, Pretty Calm:

Oh, he'll be all right. He's got a bad blow on the head, suffering from shock, mashed hands. But I can't find much other damage.

> Doctor examining a victim of the rampaging giant sea creature in *The Monster of Piedras Blancas*, 1958

On Doctors, When They're <u>Really</u> Needed:

Mr Pleyel's been murdered! Get a doctor! Quickly!

> The dead man's secretary in *Phantom of the Opera*, 1943

On Double-Dating, Literal:

Daisy: Come on, Viv, we have a date.
Viv: No, *you* have a date.
Daisy: If I have a date, you have a date, too, my dear.

> Siamese twin sisters powdering their noses in *Chained for Life*, 1951

On Double Entendres:

Aha! The Capitan's blade is not so firm, eh?

> Zorro (Tyrone Power) taunting the evil Capitan (Basil Rathbone) during a sword fight in *The Mark of Zorro*, 1940

On Double Entendres, Unintended:

How'd you like me to saddle up your old boyfriend?

> Hoyt (Troy Donahue) to Susan (Connie Stevens) – he means her horse – in *Susan Slade*, 1961

On Dramatic Moments, Driven:

Lock the kids in their rooms! The car is in the garage!

> James Brolin as the panicky dad being stalked by a 1977 Lincoln Continental in *The Car*, 1977

E

On Earthquakes, Annoying Problems with:

Earthquakes bring out the worst in some guys.

> George Kennedy rescuing a woman from a National Guardsman who has gone berserk in *Earthquake*, 1974

On Elvis Movies, Great Romantic Dialogue from:

Cynthia: Mike, I really go for you!
Mike: I'm just about to go for you!
Cynthia: Oooh. I can hardly wait!
Mike: If you're not outta here in about three seconds, I'm gonna put ya over mah knee, I'm gonna paddle your bottom until it's as red as that jalopy you're drivin'!

> Elvis Presley (Mike) and Shelley Fabares (Cynthia) in *Spinout*, 1966

On English Kings, Why They're Not Such Hot Dates:

War! War! That's all you think of, Dick Plantagenet! You burner! You pillager!

> Virginia Mayo as Lady Edith to George Sanders in *King Richard and the Crusaders*, 1954

On Epitaphs, Clichéd

She didn't die of pneumonia, she died of life.

Jean Harlow's agent, played by Red Buttons, in *Harlow*, 1965

On Erections, Debatable:

I'm erect, why aren't you?

Tony Moss in *Showgirls*, 1995

On Excuses About Your Sister, Stupid:

She was only my *half* sister.

Bad guy (Paul Smith) consoling himself after watching his partner-in-crime and sibling (Sybil Danning) die in *Jungle Warriors*, 1983

On Ex-First Ladies, Hot:

Jackie Kennedy Onassis character: You're an animal! How dare you! You bastard!

Aristotle Onassis character: God, what a woman! Let's go and make love.

Jacqueline Bisset and Anthony Quinn fighting in the thinly disguised biopic of Jackie O and her second husband in *The Greek Tycoon*, 1978

On Explanations, Insightful Medical:

It seems the more he melts, the stronger he gets.

Doctor explaining all in *The Incredible Melting Man*, 1978

Eyeballs, Interesting Observations on:

Why, it's not unlike an oyster or a grape!

The doctor-murdering lunatic (Bill Woods) eating the eyeball from a tortured cat in *Maniac*, 1934

On Eye-Talians, Mistaken Identity and:

Sadie: Say, mister! Who in the name o' Jerusalem are yuh, anyway?
Joe: Joe Skopapoulos.
Sadie: Huh?
Joe: Skopapoulos! Skopapoulos!
Sadie: Whut are yuh – I-talian?
Joe: Nah, I'm of Greek accent.

Sadie (Louise Fazenda), the hillbilly gal, meets the Greek fighter Joe Skopapoulos (Nat Pendleton) in *Swing Your Lady*, 1938

F

On Faces, Dangerous Thick:

Fatty, you with your thick face have hurt my instep.

> Chia-Liang Liu insulting his attacker, in an English subtitle in the Hong Kong kung fu film *Pedicab Driver*, 1989

On Facts, Indisputable:

Once they were men. Now they are land crabs!

> *Attack of the Crab Monsters*, 1957

On Fake Philosophy, Fatuous:

When the rabbit of chaos is pursued by the ferret of disorder through the fields of anarchy, it is time to hang your pants on the line of darkness. Whether they are clean or not.

> The Mysterious Chief (Roger Moore) making an inane (theoretically humorous) observation in *Spice World*, 1997

On Far-Out Chicks:

I know what I want. No, I don't. Yes, I do. I don't know.

> Jacqueline Bisset in a 'far-out' voice-over in *The Grasshopper*, 1969

On Felines, Frisky:

How often have I told you to keep that cat from desecrating my graves!

Mad doctor Bela Lugosi to his assistant in *Bowery at Midnight*, 1942

On Females, Ones That Come On a Little Strong:

I'm the kind of woman
not hard to understand.
I'm the one who CRACKS THE WHIP
and holds the upper hand.
I'll beat you, mistreat you
Till you quiver and quail.
The female of the species
Is more deadly than the male.

Leather-clad dominatrix Meg Myles singing a song in a nightclub in *Satan in High Heels*, 1962

On Fights with Giant Spiders, What You Say After:

Well, I've had enough of the unknown for one afternoon.

Heroine Mara Corday after facing off with a giant spider in *Tarantula*, 1955, also featuring Clint Eastwood

On First Things First:

Let us eat, *then* we will transplant the brain.

> Dr Frankenstein counselling patience to his assistant in *Frankenstein and the Monster from Hell*, 1974

On Food for Thought:

Isn't it strange how that lovely song reminds you of chicken salad?

> Ageing spinster typist Joan Crawford to her young and loony lover Cliff Robertson, about the title song in *Autumn Leaves*, 1956

On Former Presidents and First Ladies, Romantic Dialogues Between:

Girl: What are you going to do after the war?
Boy: I told you a hundred times.
Girl: I want to hear it once more.
Boy: I'm going into the surplus business. I'm going to buy up all the old mines and sell them to the man in the moon.
Girl: But there's no water on the moon!
Boy: How do you know so much about the moon?
Girl: I know a lot about it. I spend all my time looking at it when you're away. That's how it still is with me.
Boy: It's time for me to go now.

> Nancy (Reagan) and Ronald (Reagan) as the war-torn lovers in *Hellcats of the Navy*, 1957

On Frogs, Imperialistic:

TODAY the Pond!

TOMORROW the World!

Ad for *Frogs*, 1972

On Fruits, Delooscious:

Camser: What kind of jungle is this?
Kraik: I don't know, but I could learn to like it. [eating fruit] These things are looscious.
Camser: Looscious – you mean they're delooscious.
Kraik: What's the difference? Either way, they're tasty.

Bad guy Sheldon Leonard (Kraik) and henchman in *Daughter of the Jungle*, 1949

On Fun Talk in the Sack:

Whitley: Say something dirty.
Wife: Socks.
Whitley: Come on, say, say erection. Can you say erection?
Wife: I'll never say it!
Whitley: Ha ha ha!

Whitley Strieber (Christopher Walken) and his wife (Lindsay Crouse) in bed together in *Communion*, 1989

G

On Gang Leaders, Ineloquent:

Look. You're gonna get killed, or you're not gonna get killed. But you don't know shit. You don't know when you're gonna get killed, or how you're gonna get killed, and just shut. Shut.

> A Brooklyn thug leader known as the Prince (Norman Mailer) in Norman Mailer's *Wild 90*, 1967

On Getting Married, Points to Ponder:

Sally: Will you please tell me what the good doctor meant when he mentioned your old VD?
Bob: All right. If you must know, I did have it. But it's no worse than having an illegitimate child.
Sally: I think it is. Why, I . . . I'd sooner marry a leper.

> Couple in a doctor's office finding out – among other things – that her illegitimate baby won't have any effect on her new pregnancy in *Because of Eve*, 1948

On Giant Apes, Unliberated:

You goddamned chauvinist pig ape! . . . You want to eat me? Then go ahead!

> Jessica Lange as Dwan, the captive bimbo, in *King Kong*, 1976

On Girl Groups, Insightful Thoughts About:

You girls are nothing but meat up there. My girl don't tease pud for no money.

Frankie (Chris Nash) yelling at rocker-gal Julia Roberts in *Satisfaction*, 1988

On Girl Scientists, Deep Thoughts from:

Science is science, but a girl has to have her hair done.

Heroine scientist Mara Corday's final words in *Tarantula*, 1955

On Girl Talk:

Helen: I got a guy waitin' for me.
Neely: That's a switch from the fags you're usually stuck with!
Helen: At least *I* didn't have to marry one!

Helen Lawson (Susan Hayward) and Neely O'Hara (Patty Duke), two actresses sparring, in *Valley of the Dolls*, 1967

On Girls, the Same Everywhere:

Twenty-six million miles from Earth and the dolls are just the same.

The flight crew discussing the women on Venus in *Queen of Outer Space*, 1958

On Gold, Venusian Views on:

So what is so different about gold? We have much here on Venus.

Unimpressed Venusian gal Zsa Zsa Gabor in *Queen of Outer Space*, 1958

On Good Excuses to Get Out of Storming a Castle:

Oh, my stomach! It feels like there are beans in it!

Peasant complaining before the assault on the castle in *Barbarian Queen II: Empress Strikes Back*, 1992

On Good Ideas:

She's got two broken ribs, a broken jaw, and a bad concussion. We're going to keep her overnight for observation.

Savvy hospital nurse in *A Kiss Before Dying*, 1991

THE STUPIDEST PROMOTIONS

Pity the poor publicity writer. When faced with the daunting task of distinguishing his fifty-foot monster rabbit film from all those others out there, he must sit down and come up with the right words to attract viewers.

This is no easy job. But the intrepid publicity writer with the nimble mind forges ahead – and often crafts a masterpiece of excess. Replete with dreadful puns, promises of graphic titillation, and (often) allusions to larger-than-life breasts, these stupid movie promotions certainly attract attention . . . although possibly for the wrong reasons.

There is no such thing as bad publicity – or so the saying goes. This may indeed be true; however, we believe there certainly is such a thing as stupid publicity . . . as the following demonstrate.

On Youth Aflame, Startling Facts About:

STARTLING FACTS about modern girls and boys GONE WILD! And the lengths to which they go TO GET A THRILL! YOUTH AFLAME!
This is MEANT to shock you!
BECAUSE . . .
It can happen to those you love!

Trailer for *Youth Aflame*, 1959

On Choppers, Punky:

They were punks, stealing hub caps for kicks and then they went after the big stuff. Easy money. They thought they were tough until . . . But wait! . . . You see this fuel-injected, hot rod picture yourself. They call them THE CHOPPERS. Lock your cars and come and see national Champion Hot Rods in THE CHOPPERS. It's the most. It's wild! THE CHOPPERS.

The Choppers, 1961

On Taste in Film Production, Great 1950s Moments in:

Alive! He's Buried Alive! You must SEE to Believe. LOOK INTO THE GRAVE! It Will Turn Your Blood to ICE – SEE – IN PERSON! Not a movie! A MAN BURIED ALIVE! F-R-E-E! 'My Sin' Perfume to all girls who look into the grave and do not faint! (Ambulance on call for those that do!)

Ad that ran between features during the 1950s and 1960s

On Puns, Dreadful Moments in:

See Jane Russell Shake Her Tambourines . . . and Drive Cornel WILDE!

Ad for *Hot Blood*, 1956, starring Jane Russell and Cornel Wilde

On Great Dialogues with Deaf Composers, Part 1:

Don't shout, I'm not deaf!

> Composer Ludwig van Beethoven (Albert Basserman) in *The Melody Master*, 1941

On Great Dialogues with Deaf Composers, Part 2:

Huh?

> Beethoven (Albert Basserman) proving that he is deaf in *The Melody Master*, 1941

On Great Moments in Dialogue:

I don't like the sound of that sound.

> Judy Robinson (Heather Graham) in *Lost in Space*, 1998

On Great Moments in Romantic Dialogue:

Strip: I love you. Do you love me?
Trish: Strip . . .
Strip: You don't love me?
Trish: Oh, Strip . . .
Strip: I'm not good enough for you, is that it?
Trish: Strip! This is ridiculous. Oh, Strip!
Strip: When you're ready to admit you love me, you can have me, but not until.
Trish: Strip!

> Strip (John Travolta) and Trish (Lily Tomlin) in love with wires crossed in *Moment by Moment*, 1979

On Hallucinations, Rectal:

What can I say? These little blue midgets come into my house and, ha ha ha, they . . . it's ridiculous. They took me out of the house and they stuck a needle in my head and I had some sort of a rectal probe.

> Whitley Strieber (Christopher Walken), author, explaining to a psychiatrist what happened when he was abducted by aliens in *Communion*, 1989

On Head Questions, Clever Foreshadowing Moments About Later Guillotine Action and:

I'm sure they're there. . . . Oh, where is my head?

> Norma Shearer, looking for something in her closet in *Marie Antoinette*, 1938

On Hearts, Talking:

The heart has two auricles and two ventriloquists.

> Medical school professor explaining basic anatomy to his students in *Perversion*, 1978 (Brazil)

On Heart-to-Heart Talks, Maternal:

Now, Mike, let's start with the drugs and work our way up to the kidnapping and murder.

> Worried mum (Arlene Golonka) having a heart-to-heart with her son (Mike Norris, real-life son of Chuck) in *Survival Game*, 1987

On Heart-to-Heart Talks, Spousal:

Trish, we've got to talk. . . . What about the pool filter?

> Estranged husband to Trish (Lily Tomlin) in a supposedly poignant scene showing their estrangement in *Moment by Moment*, 1979

On Hebrews, Geographically Confused:

We're going to the land of milk and honey. Anybody know the way?

> A Hebrew, about to leave Egypt in *The Ten Commandments*, 1956

On Hellcats We Don't Want to Meet:

SHE TOOK ON THE WHOLE GANG! A howling hellcat humping a hot steel hog on a roaring rampage of revenge!

> Ad for *Bury Me an Angel*, 1971

On Helpful Giveaways:

UP-CHUCK CUP: KEEP IT HANDY – it may be required on short notice during the showing of *I Dismember Mama*.

Slogan on the side of paper 'up-chuck cup' given to patrons of *I Dismember Mama*, 1974

On Helpful Hints:

You *have* to listen! You have to listen to what the bees have to say!

Scientist's main squeeze Sandra (Angel Tompkins) urging everyone to listen to the killer bees' environmental message in *The Bees*, 1978

On Helping Others, Handy Hints About:

She was in great pain. Then we cut off her head and drove a stake through her heart and burned her, and then she was at peace.

Anthony Hopkins reassuring everyone in *Bram Stoker's Dracula*, 1992

On Hip Sayings, Kung Fu Style:

Jumpin' wontons!

Oriental hip guy (Victor Sen Yung) in *She Demons*, 1958

THE STUPIDEST COOL LINES

Juvenile delinquents, beatnik girls in black tights, wild-eyed hippies, and cynical '80s and '90s club kids or slackers are the purveyors of a particularly whimsical form of the stupid movie line: the cool line.

Intended to serve as evidence of the cutting-edge nature of the film, these attempts at edgy realism are marked by the heavy use of (theoretically) up-to-the-minute slang – repeated as often as possible to bludgeon us into accepting their cooler-than-thou status.

Instead, these lines remind us that sometimes it's best to leave hip as a joint in your body. Dig?

On Things We're Willing to Bet Columbus's Queen Never Said:

Christy, what is this jazz you puttin' down about our planet being round? Everybody hip that it's square!

John Drew Barrymore, paraphrasing what Queen Isabella said to Columbus, in *High School Confidential!*, 1958

On the Future:

The future is a drag, man. The future is a flake.

Beat chick in *High School Confidential!*, 1958

On Dykes, Jazzy:

Girl: Don't look at me like that. I can read your head. Dolly and Patty have nothing to do with thee and me.

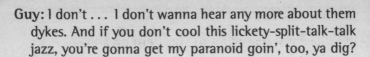

Guy: I don't . . . I don't wanna hear any more about them dykes. And if you don't cool this lickety-split-talk-talk jazz, you're gonna get my paranoid goin', too, ya dig?

Beatnik girl and boyfriend discussing two lesbians at another table in *Once a Thief*, 1965

On Digging, Dig?:

You know what I want to be? Nothing, you dig? If you can't dig 'nothing', you can't dig anything. Dig?

John Phillip Law as a hippie in *Skidoo*, 1968

On God, Cool:

If there is a God, I'd like to meet the dude, I'd like to go hang out with him.

Mickey Rourke as the biker guy in *Harley Davidson and the Marlboro Man*, 1991

On Horns, Well-Hung:

They may have bigger horns in museums, but thirty-three inches is nothing to be ashamed of.

Author/hunter Gregory Peck to Ava Gardner in *The Snows of Kilimanjaro*, 1952

On Hot Dates:

Did I love you that night or was I just an animal?

Barbara Rush telling doctor Richard Burton that he's made her preggers in *The Bramble Bush*, 1960

On Hot Volcanic Matter, Technical Definition of:

Scientist: The source of our radiation pointed to hot volcanic matter.
Explorer: You mean lava?

Rudolph Anders and Tod Griffin getting scientific in *She Demons*, 1958

On Hotels, Very Odd:

Stagecoach driver: That place – Jamaica Inn. It's got a bad name. It's not healthy, that's why. There's queer things goes on there.
Woman: Eh?
Stagecoach driver: *Queer* things. I once slept there and not a sheet was on my double bed.

Alfred Hitchcock's *Jamaica Inn*, 1939

On Houseguests Who Just Don't Quit:

It's Mrs Holden! This morning she was in her coffin in the funeral home and now she's in my kitchen!

Justifiably upset housewife in *Gates of Hell*, 1963

On How to Distract Yourself from Smog Monsters:

Great idea! We get all the hip kids we know and stage a party on Mount Fuji.

Ken's older teenage brother, planning a rock and roll party, instead of worrying about the smog monster in *Godzilla vs. the Smog Monster*, 1972

On Humans, Typical Alien Thoughts About:

These bodies are uncomfortable and fall apart in such a short time and their intelligence is low, but they do manage to enjoy themselves!

Disgruntled alien who is occupying a human body in *I Married a Monster from Outer Space*, 1958

On Hunks, Frightening:

I'm afraid of you. I've discovered you have an exciting mind, something handsome men rarely have – and the combination might be too much for me.

Career girl/virgin Maggie McNamara to playboy/art lover Louis Jourdan in *Three Coins in the Fountain*, 1954

On Hypothetical Questions by Scientists, Intriguing:

Would you allow me to come to your house and in your presence anaesthetize your wife?

Scientist to another scientist in *Unearthly Stranger*, 1964

On the Important Things in Life:

The only thing that is important is the tattooed girl! We don't spare any go-juice finding her. We don't waste it anywhere else. You cancel all those tractor pulls and all that stuff!

Deacon (Dennis Hopper) to his followers, explaining that they must find the young girl with the map on her back in *Waterworld*, 1995

On Infidels, Tricky:

Sultan Saladin: May the seven doves rest on your shoulders.
Sir Kenneth: Doves? Or vultures? You slippery infidel!

Rex Harrison and Laurence Harvey in *King Richard and the Crusaders*, 1954

On Insecurities:

I didn't mean that! Honest, I didn't! Sometimes I get too physical; it's a sign of insecurity, you know? Like when you knock down trees.

Jessica Lange as Dwan, the lady in distress, apologizing to King Kong for hurting his feelings and his nose in *King Kong*, 1976

On Insults, Confusing But Catchy:

Your incompetence sticks needles into the flesh of my honour.

Frustrated bad guy Koga Shuko (Robert Patrick), to one of his henchmen in *Double Dragon*, 1993

On Insults, Cool:

I don't mean to be insulting, babe, but I've had more action in a rocking chair.

Young (and disappointed) intern/lover-boy to the doctor's wife, Marian McCargo, in *Doctors' Wives*, 1971

On Insults, Devastating:

You'll wind up a shrivelled-up old maid or a motel tramp!

Attorney Jack Carson screaming at his former love Angie Dickinson, who has decided to leave him in *The Bramble Bush*, 1960

On Insults, Devastating Kung Fu:

Damn you, stink man!

English subtitle in *Caged Beauties*, 1988

On Insults, Fowl:

Is my husband in your chickenlike arms?

Liz Taylor as Zee yelling up to the window of Susannah York's apartment in the psychedelic *X, Y, and Zee*, 1972

On Insults, Intellectual Scientist's:

You're so bossy you ought to be milked before you come home at night!

Frustrated scientist Roy talking to the pretty Alice, who he's eventually going to marry in *Robot Monster*, 1953

On Insults, Stupid Tight Ones:

You're a sphincter muscle, Adam!

Jamie Lee Curtis fighting with John Travolta in *Perfect*, 1985

On Integrity:

I may be a liar, a cheat, a drunk, and a tramp, but I've got principles.

Joanna Cassidy as the university dean's wife protesting her innocence in *All-American Murder*, 1992

On Invisible Boys, Why They're Invisible:

Don't make such a fuss. He's probably doing this just to get attention.

Invisible boy's dad to the worried mum in *The Invisible Boy*, 1957

On IQs, Obviously High:

Girl: I've divided boys into three types – the sweepers, the strokers, and the subtles. I'll have to figure out a new classification for you.
Boy: What's your IQ?

Dolores Hart and George Hamilton as world-weary teens in *Where the Boys Are*, 1960

On Irony, Big Moments in:

Newspaper headline: 'Man Lives Through Plutonium Blast'
Thirty-Foot Colossal Man: That's a great joke, isn't it, Sergeant? [laughs] They call this living.

The Amazing Colossal Man, 1957

On It Never Happens Here, Only in Romania:

This is America, not the Carpathian Mountains!

Mad scientist (Whit Bissell) who is upset to learn that one of his 'experiments' has become a werewolf in *I Was a Teenage Werewolf*, 1957

On It Sure Does:

Sure looks bad for Dr Sorenson and the Cosmic Man, doesn't it, Mom?

Crippled little boy to his mother in *The Cosmic Man*, 1959

J

On Jet Men:

I'm a jet man, not a gigolo.

Pilot and patriot John Wayne, when asked to seduce Russian girl pilot Janet Leigh in *Jet Pilot*, 1957

On Jewish Words:

Is 'schmuck' a Jewish word? I just wanted to say something in Jewish to you.

Lucie Arnaz as Neil Diamond's manager, holding an agent at gunpoint in *The Jazz Singer*, 1980

On Jody, Hot:

This is the story of Jody . . . the kicks she digs . . . the swingers she runs with . . . and the special kind of hell she can make for a man!!!

Ad copy for *Kitten with a Whip*, 1964, starring Ann-Margret

On Joey Buttafuoco, Advantages of Dating:

He loves me. We have great sex. And he fixes my car.

Noelle Parker as Amy Fisher explaining why she's with Joey Buttafuoco in *Lethal Lolita – Amy Fisher: My Story*, 1992

On John Philip Sousa Marches, Very Sexy:

If you've never made love to 'The Stars and Stripes Forever,' you haven't lived!

Angie Dickinson, the unhappy, to Suzanne Pleshette, the soon-to-be-happy, in *Rome Adventure*, 1962

On Jokes, Clever:

Satori: I kept one piece [of the magic medallion] and hid the other where no one will ever find it.
Billy: In Jimmy's underwear?

The enlightened Satori (Julia Nickson) having a discussion with one of the not-so-enlightened but good-natured Lee brothers (Scott Wolf) in *Double Dragon*, 1993

On Jokes, Not That Clever:

Woman: Are, or are you not, going to seduce me?
Man: I are not.

Frank discussion in *Three on a Date*, 1978

On Jokes, Scrambled:

Maid: How do you want your eggs? Poached, fried, or raw?
Meade: Scrambled – like your head!

Phyllis Diller and Bob Hope in *Boy, Did I Get a Wrong Number!*, 1966

On Killing Daddy:

This is going to ruin *everything,* isn't it?

> Heiress Meg Tilly after she accidentally kills her stepfather in *Masquerade,* 1988

On Killing, Necessity of Life for:

You wouldn't kill anything unless it was alive.

> Robert Taylor speaking to Anthony Quinn in *Ride Vaquero,* 1953

On Lakes, What to Say When You See:

Boy, pointing to huge lake in front of him: Randy, is that water down there?

The Beast of Yucca Flats, 1961

On Lay-offs, When Necessary:

When a man doesn't know the difference between experimenting on an air force officer and a cadaver, I think it's time to drop him from the team.

CIA agent (Wendell Corey) discussing a problem in *Astro-Zombies*, starring John Carradine, 1967

On Leg Thieves, Common Retorts to:

Bastard! You stole my leg! Give it back immediately!

Man who keeps losing his wooden leg in the Indonesian film *Special Silencers* (no date)

On Letting Off Steam After Being Fired, Scary:

Ahhh. Royalty. Uh-huh. We parted friends. Eee-yah! Everyone already knows – box office poison. Heh-heh. Box office *poison*! CLASS . . . You're class – you're class. Box office poison. Eighteen years in the BUSINESS . . . Parted friends. EEE-UH . . . CREATIVE DIFFERENCES! [to her daughter] TINA! BRING ME THE AXE!

> Joan Crawford (Faye Dunaway) destroying her flower garden with clippers after being fired by Louis B. Mayer in *Mommie Dearest*, 1981

On Liberated Chicks:

It's *Ms* Teenager, please. I'm emancipated, liberated, and highly skilled in kung fu.

> Young stewardess objecting to being called a 'teenager' in *Airport 1975*, 1974

On Life After Death, Mums and:

If your mother were alive, she'd turn over in her grave!

> Anthony Quinn telling it like it is to John Turturro in *Jungle Fever*, 1991

On Life, Deep Thoughts on:

The world is a strange place to live in. All those cars! All going someplace! All carrying humans which are carrying out their lives! . . . But life, even though its changes are slow, moves on.

> Narrator 1, the psychiatrist (Timothy Farrell), commenting on the passing scene in *Glen or Glenda?*, 1953

WHEN BAD LINES HAPPEN
TO GOOD ACTORS

It happens to the best of them – actors who, faced with a new mortgage on their seventh house or in dire need of a tax write-off, find themselves forced to utter terrible lines with a totally straight face.

This may be bad luck for them, but it is a boon for the viewer – who can be mesmerized by the sight of Shakespearean actors declaiming about killer frogs, Oscar-winners emoting about chicken salad, and, of course, histrionics about wire hangers.

These lines are so noxious they might literally poison the careers of lesser actors. Here, then, are some lines that packed large doses of poison, but fortunately not enough to destroy the careers of these famous lights of the silver screen.

On Admissions, Shocking:

We made love – even in motels, God help me!

Richard Burton confessing infidelity to his wife in *The Sandpiper*, 1965

On Wire Hangers, Final Words on:

No wire HANGERS! What's wire hangers doing in this closet when I told you NO WIRE HANGERS *EVER*!

Faye Dunaway as Joan Crawford after finding wire clothes hangers in her daughter's closet in *Mommie Dearest*, 1981

On Bees, Turncoat:

I never would have dreamed it would turn out to be the bees! They've always been our friends!

Michael Caine in *The Swarm*, 1978

On Scientific Dialogue, Great Moments in:

Bzzz. Bzzz. Bzzz.

Scientist Henry Fonda trying to have a little chat with some angry bees in *The Swarm*, 1978

On Life's Little Problems:

Daughter: I was in an orgy. I was a stripper. I was a streetwalker. Then in a motel a man tried to forcibly seduce me.
Mother: There, there, dear. If you think these things are bad, wait till your children grow up.

Ann-Margret talking to mum in *The Swinger*, 1966

On, Like, Problems:

Dad's all torn up and Mom's got, like, a harpoon in her neck.

Boy explaining the problems with the aliens at home to the police in *Critters*, 1986

On Like, What Does It, Like, Remind You of . . . :

Well, the cross makes me think death, but the ivy is, like, sort of, the tragic and the hopeful, you know?

Ivy (Drew Barrymore) explaining why she has a cross and some ivy tattooed on her body in *Poison Ivy*, 1992

On Lines That Are Tough to Deliver with a Straight Face:

Kokumo can help me find Pazuzu!

Priest (Richard Burton) naming the African healer who will help him find the Evil One in *Exorcist II: The Heretic*, 1977

On Little Boys:

And what are little boys made of? Is it snakes and snails and puppy dog tails? Or is it brassieres! And corsets!

Narrator in *Glen or Glenda?*, 1953

On Little Sisters, Good Points About:

I'm afraid the world doesn't look at a sixty-foot man the way a sister does.

Army officer (Roger Pace) trying to break some news to the sister of an unnaturally large man in *War of the Colossal Beast*, 1958

On Logic, Colossal:

Major Baird: That's a big footprint!
Dr Carmichael: The foot that made that print is about ten times the size of a normal man.
Major Baird: That would make him about sixty feet tall.
Joyce: Glen was sixty feet tall!

Sister of the giant man (Sally Fraser) and the authorities (Roger Pace and Russ Bender) examining a gigantic footprint and coming to some astonishing conclusions, in *War of the Colossal Beast*, 1958

On Lost Loves, Great Memories of:

We never did find the gold, but we had something better: my Jack had all the nuggets we needed right between his legs.

Helena Kallianiotes as demented mining town madam Frieda, mourning her lost lover in *Eureka*, 1981

On Love, Not Enough Pollination and:

I'm fed up with being an undeflowered wife!

Karin Schubert as a soon-to-be-dead wife complaining to husband (and soon-to-be-murderer) Richard Burton in *Bluebeard*, 1972

M

On Mad Doctors, Why Not to Get Them Irritated:

I'd like to rip your ****ing skull off, but instead I'll make you permanently insane!

Mad doctor to pesky patient in *Hellhole*, 1985

On Mad Scientists, Dull:

Well, as a scientist I am more interested in things with six legs than two. No doubt I am in the minority.

Mad scientist (George Colouris) explaining his apparent lack of interest in women to cop in *Womaneater*, 1957

On Mad Scientists, Handy Rationalizations for:

If this guy had been healthy, he'd still be alive now!

Bruce Dern, the scientist, explaining things to another scientist in *The Incredible Two-Headed Transplant*, 1971

On Maggots, Complicated:

Doctor: You know, I've been working for years, developing, breeding, and conditioning these maggots . . . They feed on human flesh.

Nazi: Why must it be human flesh? Why not animal?

Doctor: I haven't got time to explain it to you now.

Veronica Lake (the doctor) and Phil Philbin as the Nazi, discussing her new scientific breakthrough in *Flesh Feast*, 1970

On Male-Female Ageing, Similarities of:

Girl: In five years I'll be older:

Boy: So will I.

Cynthia Gibb and Burt Reynolds in *Malone*, 1987

On Martian Guys, Horny:

Space officer: Well, what did you decipher? . . . Let's have it!

Space technician: It's just three words.

Space officer: I didn't ask for a word count, just give me the message!

Space technician: We've checked and double-checked. It keeps coming up to the same thing. The message is 'MARS NEEDS WOMEN!'

Airforce decoder to his colonel after deciphering a message from Mars in *Mars Needs Women*, 1968

On Medical Speculation, Logical:

I've never heard of a healthy person dropping dead just because he had the desire to do so.

Suspicious doctor examining a body in *The Curse of the Doll People*, 1961

On Melting Friends, What to Say to:

Oh, my God! You look awful!

Scientist to his melting friend in *Food of the Gods II*, 1988

On Metaphors, Mystifying:

I got knife scars more than the number of your leg's hair!

Not-so-great English subtitle in Hong Kong kung fu film *As Tears Go By*, 1988

On Metaphors, New:

Don't be afraid of Lobo. He's as harmless as a kitchen.

Scientist Bela Lugosi to the trembling girl heroine in *Bride of the Monster*, 1953 (reportedly, Lugosi was having drug problems and refused to correct the line to 'harmless as a kitten')

THE STUPIDEST ALIEN LINES

Aliens and monsters in film are often saddled with the most difficult task of all – to spout ostensibly threatening lines while parading about in a plastic costume . . . or (for the disembodied brain-type of monster) while floating in a glass jar or occupying an uncomfortable human body.

To complicate matters, said alien or monster must also speak in a manner appropriately alien or monsterlike on matters uniquely alien or monsterlike. This becomes especially problematic in the films exploring the convoluted love triangles with hideous monster, handsome young scientist, and woman (typically in the requisite 1950s pointy rocket-shaped bra). A fascinating question about interstellar sexual practices inevitably arises: why do male alien monsters so often fall for young 1950s women, instead of females of their own kind? The incongruities of, for example, a giant, floating, alien brain named Gor lusting after a big-breasted woman with pointy rocket-shaped bra instead of a cute female alien brain makes for dialogue that borders on the absolutely ludicrous.

However, whatever the plight of the alien or monster, we can rest assured that – regardless of its form or interests – something monstrously stupid is bound to come out of its mouth (or gill . . . or temporal lobe . . .).

On Evil Brains, Choosy:

I chose your body very carefully. Even before I knew about Sally . . . a *very* exciting female.

Gor, the evil alien brain who has taken over scientist Dr Steve March's (John Agar's) body, in *The Brain from Planet Arous*, 1958

On Robot Monsters, Fascinating Dialogue from:

Great One: Have you made the correction?

Ro-Man: I need guidance, Great One. For the first time in my life, I am not sure.

Great One: You sound like a hu-man, not a Ro-Man. Can you not verify a fact?

Ro-Man: I meshed my LP1 with the viewscreen auditor, and picked up a count of five.

Great One: Error! Error! There are eight!

Ro-Man: Then the other three still elude me. And all escape detection by the directional bearer. Is it possible they have a counterpower?

Robot Monster, 1953

On Military Questions, Important:

Houston on fire . . . Will history blame me – or the bees?

The General (Richard Widmark) pondering in *The Swarm*, 1978

On Military Reasoning:

Scientist: It's weird. Why don't we see anyone? What happened to everybody who was hurt or killed?

Soldier: I think I know what happened. Frankenstein got hungry and they were just available.

Explanation as to where all the bodies went in *Frankenstein Conquers the World*, 1966

On Moments, Bad:

A head without a body! A head that should be in its grave!
Let me die! Let me die!

> Virginia Leith, Jan the mad scientist's decapitated fiancée, in
> *The Brain That Wouldn't Die*, 1962

On Mums, Hungry:

Girlfriend: Your mother ate my dog.
Boyfriend: Not all of it.

> Girlfriend (Diana Peñalver) to boyfriend (Timothy Balme)
> whose mother has been bitten by Sumatran rat monkeys and
> has got a craving for undead flesh in *Dead Alive*, 1992 (also
> known as *Braindead*)

On Moses, Adorable:

Oh, Moses, Moses, you stubborn, splendid, adorable fool!

> Nefretiri (Anne Baxter) to Moses (Charlton Heston) in *The Ten
> Commandments*, 1956

On Moses, Body Odour and:

They may be your people, but do you have to wallow with
them . . . *smell* like them?

> Nefretiri to Moses in *The Ten Commandments*, 1956

On Mother, Not Herself:

Aunt Patience: Mary! Mary! My sweet, sweet Mary! . . . Mary! You're in black!
Mary: Yes. . . . Mother died three weeks ago.
Aunt Patience: How did it happen?
Mary: She hadn't been well. . . . You know how mother was.

Maureen O'Hara as Mary and Marie Ney as Aunt Patience in Hitchcock's *Jamaica Inn*, 1939

On Mottoes, Different:

If you don't eat people, they'll eat you.

Motto of cannibals from Cannibal Island in *We Are Going to Eat You*, 1980 (Hong Kong)

On Movie Ads, Believable:

WARNING: This is John Austin Frazier. It has been reported that he now resides at a Mental Hospital, the result of attending our triple horror programme. Because of this tragic event, we, the producers, have secured an insurance policy insuring the sanity of each and every patron. If you lose your mind as a result of viewing this explosion of terror, you will receive *free* psychiatric care or be placed *at our expense* in an asylum for the rest of your life!

Newspaper ad showing a demented-looking man, for the movie triple bill *Fangs of the Living Dead*, 1968, *Revenge of the Living Dead*, 1972, and *Curse of the Living Dead*, 1966

N

On Natives, Hip:

Real crazy. These footprints go in a circle. Maybe the natives here are getting on this rock 'n' roll kick.

Oriental hip guy (Victor Sen Yung) when he and his buddies discover sinister footprints on the desert island they're stranded on in *She Demons*, 1958

On Neurotics, Typical:

Major's wife: Cutting off her nipples with garden shears? You call *that* normal?
Colonel: Well, the doctors say she's neurotic.

Army base conversation between Elizabeth Taylor and Brian Keith after Keith's wife miscarries and then cuts off her nipples in *Reflections in a Golden Eye*, 1967

On Nipples, Buoyant:

I want my nipples to press, but I don't want them to look like they're levitating.

Showgirl in *Showgirls*, 1995

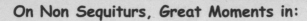

On Non Sequiturs, Great Moments in:

James: Your brother's dead.
Nonnie (tearily): Did you like his music?

> Red Buttons and Carol Lynley having a conversation over her brother's body in *The Poseidon Adventure*, 1972

On Nude Moon Women, Stupid Paper-Eating:

Earthman (in a very bad space suit, talking to a nude moon woman): Hello. I saw you on the throne before. You must be the queen. I've brought something for you. On Earth we call this candy.
[He gives her some candy in wax paper. She spits out the candy and eats the wrapper.]
Earthman: Ha, ha – ha, ha – ho, ho – You're not supposed to eat the paper.

> From *Nude on the Moon*, 1962

On Nurses, Bad Diagnostic Abilities of:

Every bone in his body must be broken, but I'm not sure that's what killed him.

> Nurse Ann Doran examining a returning astronaut and realizing Earthlings are in for trouble in *It! The Terror from Beyond Space*, 1958

O

On Oh-So-Cute Lines:

You know something, Doctor? I'm not going to worry about overpopulation just yet.

> Charter-boat captain (James Best) kissing the population scientist doctor's daughter and Best's bride-to-be in *The Killer Shrews*, 1959

On the Old Brainwash:

Catlett: If Olmstead is alive there is a chance the enemy may find ways to make him talk!
Tom: The old brainwash!
Catlett: Exactly.

> George Cisar and John Agar as heroic jet flyboys during the Korean War in *Jet Attack*, 1958

On the Old Masters, Exasperatingly Indecisive:

Michelangelo, make up your mind, once and for all: Do you want to finish that ceiling?

> *The Agony and the Ecstasy*, 1965, starring Charlton Heston as Michelangelo

On One for Each Eye:

See Jane Russell in 3-D; She'll Knock Both Your Eyes Out!

Ad for *The French Line*, 1954

On Ooga Bonga, Meaning of:

Native Chief: Ooga bonga dongay!
Jack: He wants to make a deal. Six of them for Dwan.
Dwan: Jack, can you tell him I like him too, but not *that* way?

Dwan (Jessica Lange) explaining to Jack (Jeff Bridges) that she doesn't want to be traded to the savage native chief in *King Kong*, 1976

On Opening Lines, Enigmatic:

Pull the string! Pull the string! Life has begun! A story must be told!

Narrator 2 (Bela Lugosi) in *Glen or Glenda?*, 1953

On Orders, Hard to Follow:

Suck the coffin mushroom now.

The Ultimate Vampire, 1991

P

On Pain and Suffering, Beyond the Pale:

It's bad enough having no immune system, but having to wear this giant cabbage on my head is too much.

John Travolta as a boy with a rare immune disorder in the tear-jerker, disease-of-the-week film *The Boy in the Plastic Bubble*, 1976

On Paleontology, Essential Facts About:

Dr Blake: Do you know anything about paleontology?
Molly: I know that very attractive men study it.

Professor and young student, in *Monster on the Campus*, 1958

On Parties, Downers at:

Him: The food has been cooked, the wines chilled . . .
Her: And the guest of honour's on the bottom of the lake.

Rock Hudson and Dorothy Malone commiserating over the fact that her pilot husband has just crashed his plane instead of coming to his party in *Tarnished Angels*, 1957

On Past-Life Experiences, Bad:

Ow! I'm shot!

Lyle Wheeler (Marjoe Gortner) reliving a past life as Billy the Kid under the influence of peyote in *Bobbie Jo and the Outlaw*, 1976

On Past-Life Memories, Fuzzy:

Psychiatrist: What is your name?

Hypnotized patient: Laura Carson.

Psychiatrist: Go on . . .

Hypnotized patient: Angora sweater – was such a beautiful thing. Soft, like kitten's fur. Felt so good on me. As if it belonged there. Felt so bad when it was gone.

Psychiatrist: Dan, do you realize we've just witnessed a portion of your wife's previous existence? . . . Her talk about maribou, Angora, and furlike materials . . . I believe that it's derived from her past existence.

Dan: Aw, come on. You don't really believe she was a gorilla?

Psychiatrist: All the evidence points to it. Her fixation for furlike materials comes from that fact.

Dan: I'm sorry, Doctor, I just don't buy any of this.

Psychiatrist: Well, you have a right to your own opinion.

Psychiatrist (William Justine) takes patient (Charlotte Austin) back to her past life as a gorilla. Unfortunately, her husband (Lance Fuller) doesn't buy it in *The Bride and the Beast*, 1958

On Pat Boone Lines, Typical:

Emily: I've been around.
Wayne: Does that mean you're a bad girl?

Ann-Margret and Pat Boone in *State Fair*, 1962

On Patriotism:

We're hoodlums - but we're American hoodlums!

Frank Jenks as Jimbo, an escaped con, dealing with Nazis in
Seven Miles from Alcatraz, 1942

On Peace, Need for No War in:

If we are to live together in peace, there must be no war
between us!

George Chakiris as Balam getting down to the real nitty gritty,
to Yul Brynner as Chief Black Eagle in *Kings of the Sun*, 1963

On Penises, Glaringly Obvious Puns and:

Let's see how it stands up in the light of day.

Surgical nurse after the operation in the penis-transplant
comedy *Percy*, 1971, starring Denholm Elliott and Britt
Ekland

On Philosophy Degrees, What You Learn with:

Man's search for faith, that sort of shit.

Cool bouncer Patrick Swayze explaining what he learned
while getting his philosophy degree, to Kelly Lynch in *Road
House*, 1989

On Pick-up Lines, One of the Worst:

Is it just me or does the jungle make you really, really horny?

> Owen Wilson, as documentary sound mixer Gary in the Amazon jungle, to his co-worker in *Anaconda*, 1997

On Plants, Smart 'n' Sassy:

Plants are the most cunning of all life forms!

> Doc Roller (Bernard Kates) in *Seedpeople*, 1992

On Pleas, Heartfelt:

I don't want to be killed! I just want to teach English.

> Panicking actor in the TV movie *Echoes in the Darkness*, 1987

On the Pleasures of Life:

Texan: A little poontang might ease your mind a bit.
Cochran: I killed a man I hated today.
Texan: I got ya. You don't want to mix your pleasures.

> James Gammon (Texan) and Kevin Costner (Cochran) as two down-and-outers bent on revenge against Anthony Quinn in *Revenge*, 1990

THE STUPIDEST QUASI-INTELLECTUAL MOVIE LINES

Hollywood, many insiders say, is not the most intellectual of places. People spend their free time in pursuits other than talking about the meaning of life or what Spinoza really meant.

Yet, all too often, a film character is called upon to say something (theoretically) profound. How can one be sure that the not-terribly-profound profundity is adequately appreciated by the audience?

Often screenwriters take the simplest route – have one character say the erstwhile profound line, then have the next character reply by saying something such as, 'That was very profound.' (This, of course, is designed to tip off any confused viewers.)

Other screenwriters – particularly those who believe in their own mighty intellectualism – opt for the more highbrow: a character spouts forth a slew of random words and thoughts, most often in a bored manner. The savvy viewer will notice that these lines make no sense. This is the vital clue that something profound was just said.

In either case, the results, if not thought-provoking, are singularly laughter-provoking.

On Ugliness, Wisdom About:

Ugly bad guy: Maybe if man is ugly, he does ugly things.
Plastic surgeon: You are saying something profound.

Boris Karloff (ugly guy) and Bela Lugosi (surgeon) having a discussion in *The Raven*, 1935

On Existential Observations About Hotel Hallways:

Once again everything was deserted in the immense hotel. Empty salons, corridors, salons, doors, doors, salons . . . empty chairs, deep armchairs . . . stairs, steps, steps one after another . . . glass objects, empty glasses . . . a dropped glass, a glass partition . . . letters, a lost letter . . . keys hanging from their rings . . . marked door keys, 309, 307, 305, 303 . . . chandeliers, chandeliers, pearls, mirrors . . . corridors without a soul in sight . . . and the garden, like all else, was deserted.

Fascinating monologue delivered by the intense young man X (Giorgio Albertazzi) intent on finding a woman he might have known, in *Last Year at Marienbad*, 1962

On Dialogue, Anyway but Good:

There's a thousand sides to everything, not just heroes and villains. . . . So anyway . . . so anyway . . . so anyway . . . 'So anyway' ought to be one word. Like a place or a river.

Daria Halprin, a far-out young woman in *Zabriskie Point*, 1970

On Points about Godzilla, Pretty Obvious:

This thing is much too big to be some lost dinosaur.

Dr Niko Tatopoulus (Matthew Broderick), in *Godzilla*, 1998

On Points, Debatable:

It's better to be dead and cool than alive and unc

> Said by both Mickey Rourke and Don Johnson as the ultra-cool biker boy and the hip cowboy in *Harley Davidson and the Marlboro Man*, 1991

On Points to Ponder:

Novice bartender: The waitresses hate me.
Old-hand bartender: Wait till you've given them crabs – then you'll really know hatred.

> Tom Cruise and Bryan Brown in *Cocktail*, 1988

On Poison, Problems with:

Louise was feeling good until you gave her that poison.

> The detective (Stuart Whitman) making a sinister observation about his sister's death to the doctor (Martin Landau) in *Strange Shadows in an Empty Room*, 1976

On Police Intelligence:

This criminal must be found. Otherwise, these acts will continue!

> Very smart cop in *Rock 'n' Roll Wrestling Women vs. the Aztec Ape*, 1962

Pornography, Succinct Thoughts On:

Pornography. It's a nasty word for a dirty business.

Detective Kenne Duncan summing up the movie in *The Sinister Urge*, 1960

On Premarital Sex, the Price of:

Poor kid! Maybe this is the price you pay for sleeping together.

Rock Hudson, to the camera, as Jennifer Jones dies in childbirth in *A Farewell to Arms*, 1957

On Pretentious Convicted Killers, Statements from:

Mendacity is the great sin that's destroying America, and I'm a living reproach to you 'cause I'm an honest man.

Mickey Rourke as a convicted killer holding a family hostage in *Desperate Hours*, 1990

On a Pretty Bad Morning:

Then, one morning I woke up, the sun was shining . . . Jack was dead, dead inside me, dead in bed. That must have been when I started to smell bad.

Helena Kallianiotes as Frieda, the demented mining town madam, mourning her lost love in *Eureka*, 1981

On Priorities:

Jack: Listen. There's a girl out there who might be running for her life from some gigantic turned-on ape!

Fred: Jack, I know how you feel. I feel the same. But there's a national energy crisis which demands that we all rise above our private selfish interests.

Fred the expedition leader (Charles Grodin) explaining to Jack the concerned scientist (Jeff Bridges) why he can't spare the men to go and save Jessica Lange as Dwan from King Kong, in *King Kong*, 1976

On Problems, Getting to the Heart of:

It's in a doll. Unfortunately, I can't find the doll.

Man (Robert Culp) explaining what's happened to his heart in *Spectre*, 1977

On Problems, Problems:

Mike Brady: We have a very serious situation on our hands here.

Businessman: Situation? What kind of situation?

Mike Brady: This entire area used to be a toxic waste dump. And not only that, we have a mutant form of killer slug in our water system!

Health Inspector Mike Brady (Michael Garfield) explaining some of the problems of doing business in his town to a businessman in *Slugs*, 1988

On Psychos, Problems of:

Why is it I always gotta kill somebody to get them to take me seriously?

Misunderstood psycho Kevin Dillon in *Misbegotten*, 1997

On Public Service Announcements We Hope We Never Hear:

The survival command centre at the Pentagon has disclosed that a ghoul can be killed by a shot in the head. . . . Officials are quoted as explaining that since the brain of a ghoul has been activated by the radiation, the plan is: Kill the brain and you kill the ghoul!

TV newsman giving the world some hope in *Night of the Living Dead*, 1968

On Publicity Problems, Monsters and:

We can't let them out into the city. All they would have to do is eat a couple of small children and we would have the most appalling publicity.

Scientist (Christopher Lee) explaining the problem in *Gremlins 2: The New Batch*, 1990

On Puns, Large:

You know what they wrote about me in the high school yearbook? The man most likely to reach the top!

The really tall colossal man talking to his fiancée in *The Amazing Colossal Man*, 1957

Q

On Queens, Potentially Fecund:

My breasts are full of love and life. My hips are round and well apart. Such women, they say, have sons.

Cleopatra (Elizabeth Taylor) seducing Caesar (Rex Harrison) in *Cleopatra*, 1963

On Questions About the Neighbours, Intriguing:

How many of our neighbours have their girlfriends' heads in their freezers?

Wife of philandering husband Peter Gallagher in *Virtual Obsession*, 1998

On Questions, Good:

We sold our bodies; why can't we sell some wood?

Interesting question posed by liberated western gal soon-to-be-entrepreneur in *Bad Girls*, 1994, starring Andie MacDowell, Drew Barrymore, Madeleine Stowe and Mary Stuart Masterson

On Questions Often Asked by Semi-nude Native Women:

Kiss? What is kiss?

Scantily-clad island woman getting to know a washed-ashore sailor in *Pagan Island*, 1960

On Questions, Oh-So-Cosmic:

Is one happier, do you think, with ten years of happiness than if one has ten minutes or ten days?

Jane Fonda as the young girl in love with Peter Finch in *In the Cool of the Day*, 1963

On Questions, Questions:

Where are my tits? Where are my tits!?

Myron (Rex Reed) waking up in the hospital in *Myra Breckinridge*, 1970

On Questions, Shocking:

You used your own granddaughter to give birth to a race of army elves?

Shocked department-store Santa asking a question of a Nazi scientist who has been doing some naughty experiments in *Elves*, 1989

On Questions, Unanswerable, Part 1:

What type of women are these, who attack men and live in trees?

Narrator in the prehistoric love-story movie *Prehistoric Women*, 1950

On Questions, Unanswerable, Part 2:

Give me a sign if you're still alive!

Confused prospector to his partner who is stuck full of arrows in *Revenge of the Virgins*, 1962

On Questions We Bet You Can't Answer:

WHAT'S THE SECRET INGREDIENT USED BY THE MAD BUTCHER FOR HIS SUPERB SAUSAGES?

Ad for *Meat Is Meat*, 1971

On Questions We've Never Asked:

How many people do you know can cross the Atlantic with only a hunk of salami as luggage?

Patti Page (playing herself) to Louella Parsons discussing a brave little Italian orphan in *Dondi*, 1961

On Questions We've Never Been Asked:

Have you ever been collared and dragged out in the street and thrashed by a naked woman?

Elizabeth Taylor as a frustrated wife in *Reflections in a Golden Eye*, 1967

R

On Race Relations, Head Transplantation Problems with:

Doctor: Max, listen to me. We did it. We transplanted your head. We did it, Max. And everything is checking out properly. Max, it's going to work.

Max (regaining consciousness): I knew it would. My God, I knew it would! I can feel it. I can breathe with it. I can feel my hand. I . . . I think I'm moving it. I think I'm lifting my left arm. I *am* lifting it. I know I am.

Doctor: Max, we had to make a last-minute decision. We had no choice.

Max (raising his hand – and seeing that it's black): Is this some kind of a joke?

Doctor talking to white bigot Ray Milland as he is waking up after the operation that transplanted his head onto Rosey Grier's (the African-American football player turned actor) body, *The Thing with Two Heads*, 1972

On Radio Messages, Unexpected:

This is God. I'll be with you for the next few days.

Radio message in *The Next Voice You Hear*, 1950

On Real Bitches:

To have no eyes means to be half a man. To have no eyes and no money – that's a bitch!

Tony Anthony, the blind cowboy in *Blindman*, 1971

On Real Bitches, Scientific:

We're scientists. We *have* to do things we hate!

Scientist Brian Donlevy in *The Curse of the Fly*, 1965

On Real Estate Developers, Post-Apocalyptic:

If there's a river, we'll dam it. If there's a tree, we'll ram it. 'Cause I'm talkin' progress here. Yes, sir! I'm talkin' development! We shall suck and savour the sweet flavour of DRY LAND!

Deacon (Dennis Hopper) exhorting his bad guy followers not only to find Dry Land but to destroy it in *Waterworld*, 1995

On Reasoning, Impeccably Logical:

When the wife of a warden of a prison talks him into getting a parole for one of the convicts, then runs off and marries that convict, you get to hate a lot of people, especially convicts.

Unhappy prison warden Andrew Duggan to a girl inmate in *House of Women*, 1962

On Romantic Dialogue, Great Monster Moments in:

Man: I'd like to take you out in a monster-free city.
Woman: I'd like that.

> Discussion between man and woman as they look out of the skyscraper window at a giant flying monster on a nest in *Gamera: Guardian of the Universe*, 1995

On Romantic Dialogue, Pretentious:

Drama coach next door: I don't know how to feel what I'm feeling when I don't even know your name.
Woman in hiding: People never really know each other.

> Kevin Anderson falling in love with Julia Roberts, who is hiding from her psycho husband, in *Sleeping with the Enemy*, 1991

On Romantic Lines, Nauseating:

Don: We'll never meet again?
Lyda: There's never any never. Kiss me.

> Troy Donahue and Angie Dickinson as unhappy lovers in *Rome Adventure*, 1962

On Root Vegetables:

An intelligent carrot – the mind boggles.

> Douglas Spencer in *The Thing*, 1951

S

On Sabu, Problems with the Word 'Fiancée' (Not to Mention Verb Tenses . . .):

I are here to look for my friend's almost wife.

Sabu in *Cobra Woman*, 1944

On Salads, Tough:

Wow! That's the first time a salad's ever tossed me!

Private Philbrick (Bob Ball) after a fight with a giant alien carrot in *Invasion of the Star Creatures*, 1962

On Schizo Stalkers, Typical Statements from:

We were both waiting for you: myself and I!

Schizophrenic stalker Bruno (Jenn LeClerc) to his intended victim in *Whispers*, 1989

On Scientific Discoveries Made While Battling Devil Girls from Mars:

So there *is* a fourth dimension.

The Professor making a discovery in *Devil Girl from Mars*, 1954

On Scientific Logic, Dry:

Actually, there was no blood. That accounts for the shrivelled effect.

Scientists examining dead body that has been killed by the nine-foot-tall mutant astronaut in *Monster a-Go Go*, 1965

On Scientist Lovers, Witty Lines from:

Although women are made up of mostly water, with a few pinches of salt and some metallic trace elements, you have a distinctly unsalty and non-metallic effect on me!

Scientist hero (Jock Mahoney) seducing his lady love in *The Land Unknown, 1957*

On Scientists, Excessively Sensitive:

I understand what that whale is feeling, 'cause the same thing happened to me.

Richard Harris comparing himself to the killer whale that lost its wife and child in *Orca*, 1977

On Sex, Moments We'd Rather Not Think About:

You think I might find happiness in the animal kingdom, Duckie?

Beverly (Lea Thompson) crawling into bed with a giant cigar-smoking duck in *Howard the Duck*, 1986

On Sexologists, Typical Thoughts from:

Why not run off with the swinging wife of the swinging director and knock off a piece! Lovemaking to you is like a stallion mounting a mare. Real people make love with their minds and their understanding, not just with their bodies!

Tippi Hedren as the sexologist at college, to young stud Don Johnson in *The Harrad Experiment*, 1973

On the Simple Things in Life, Nuclear Holocaust Style:

It's great to eat under an open sky, even if it is radioactive.

Frankie Avalon enjoying a picnic with the family in after-the-nuclear-holocaust Los Angeles in *Panic in the Year Zero*, 1962

On Sins, Angry:

We've experienced death and somehow we've brought our sins back, and they're pissed.

Scientist Kiefer Sutherland after coming back from the dead in *Flatliners*, 1990

THE STUPIDEST ATTEMPTS AT HISTORICAL DIALOGUE

How did people talk in bygone days? This is a burning question that has long plagued Hollywood. Lacking tape recordings from biblical times, ever-resourceful screenwriters have been forced to hypothesize, and two distinct schools of thought seem to have evolved:

1. The Classic School: In the past, people apparently spoke as though they were walking thesauri. They were prone to using unwieldy words ('abjure,' 'bereft,' 'hardihood,' and the like), stilted syntax (always heavy on compound verbs), and convoluted sentences (replete with dependent clause upon dependent clause). Declamation was extremely popular, as was speaking as though one were not completely comfortable with the use of action verbs.

2. The Modern School: In the past, people apparently were hip New York/LA types, and talked and acted exactly like New York/LA film people. Great figures like Moses, Columbus, and Washington were more concerned with looking cool than with saving their people or discovering new lands. They used words like 'hip,' 'drag,' 'dig' (if it was a 1960s film), or 'bitch,' 'dude,' 'awesome' (if it was a 1990s film), and posed a lot, as if they were aware that someday someone would come along and film them. In most cases, everyone has styled hair, which was, of course, the big thing from biblical times onward.

In either case, the result is more hysterical than historical, as the following demonstrate.

On Biblical Chitchat, Common:

Abjure this woman and her idolatries. Tear down the obscene abomination she has erected!

An elder to King Solomon in *Solomon and Sheba*, 1959, starring Yul Brynner and Gina Lollobrigida

On Romantic Dialogue, Great Moments in:

Genghis Khan: I shall keep you, Bortai. I shall keep you unresponding to my passion. Your hatred will kindle into love.
Bortai: Before that day dawns, Mongol, the vultures will feast on your heart!

John Wayne and Susan Hayward in *The Conqueror*, 1956

On Things We're Willing to Bet Columbus's Men Never Said:

It's not just about how far we've come, it's this bitch of a wind.

Andy Robert Davi, the captain of the *Pinta*, to Columbus in *Christopher Columbus: The Discovery*, 1992, starring Georges Corraface

On Sludge Monsters, Weakness of:

Dr Yano: In each creature a weakness exists.
Ken: Hedorah's only sludge – we could dry it out!

The scientist and his young son discussing ways to rid the world of the smog monster in *Godzilla vs. The Smog Monster*, 1972

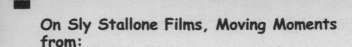

On Sly Stallone Films, Moving Moments from:

Did you bump uglies with my sister?

From the Sylvester Stallone-Kurt Russell buddy film *Tango and Cash*, 1989

On Song Lines, Utterly Banal:

I'm just the total of what I've become.

Song in *The Harrad Experiment*, 1973

On Soundtracks, How to Cover Up Problems with:

The sergeant, a shaken man, returned babbling about what had happened. Colonel Caldwell, realizing the full danger of the situation, decided that he had only one means left to top the monster: grenades! Now Professor Bradford made a drastic move. Acting on his superior authority, he forbade Caldwell to destroy the creature. The colonel, more concerned with saving lives than advancing science, told Bradford to go to hell.

Narrator in a scene in which the dialogue was apparently unusable in *The Creeping Terror*, 1964

On Space, Good Points About:

There's a lot of space out there to get lost in.

Dr John Robinson (William Hurt) in *Lost in Space*, 1998

On Spelling Problems, Bo Derek and:

... ecstasy. What a beautiful word: E-X-T- ...

Bo Derek misspelling 'ecstasy' (unless she was talking about the hip eighties drug 'extasy')' in *Bolero*, 1984

On Stomach Problems, Communist:

You're in a fine state! God, has someone cut your tongue off? Why do you get like this? Is it the altitude in – or is it something you've eaten?

Gita (Romy Schneider) to her silent boyfriend in *The Assassination of Trotsky*, 1972

On Strippers, Politically Correct:

We hate these. They degrade women and beavers.

Stripper Erin Grant (Demi Moore), protesting at the design on the coasters and napkins at the 'Eager Beaver Bar' to the manager in *Striptease*, 1996

On Studs, Real Sensitive:

I'd like to meet the kid that I was when I was five years old, because I think he's the only person on the planet who knows who I really am.

Sensitive (and satisfied) stud Don Johnson after finally making it with nice girl Laurie Walters in *The Harrad Experiment*, 1973

On Stupid Sex Descriptions:

Sex is a pleasant, friendly thing, like shaking hands or making sure you catch a person's name when you're introduced.

> George Hamilton as an on-the-make Ivy Leaguer trying to seduce Dorothy Hart in *Where the Boys Are*, 1960

On the Super-H-Bomb, Angelic Comments About:

First angel: Some devilish fellow down on the earth has actually discovered the secret of the super-H-bomb!

Second angel: That's impossible! The super-H-bomb is not scheduled for invention by the Devil until the year ... let's see ... until ... here it is ... until the year 2016. Why, they're not ready or wise enough to handle it yet. According to our heavenly statistics, if exploded now, the bomb would blow Man and his earth sky-high. No one would be left alive ... everyone would be dead.

First angel: My, my, the housing shortage up here would be terrible! What'll we do?

> Opening sequence, *The Story of Mankind*, 1957

On Supermodels, Useful:

Besides being one of our top models, she could be most helpful to our government.

> South Vietnamese colonel urging the Green Berets to make use of the beautiful Miss Saigon (Irene Tsu) in *The Green Berets*, 1968

On the Supersonic Age, Typical Problems in:

Dr Chapman: After her marriage, her health seemed to rise and fall with the tide of her emotions.

Other Doctor: Ah, a sad case. A case not infrequent in this supersonic age we live in.

Two doctors discussing the problems of the alcoholic woman who has become fifty feet tall in *Attack of the 50 Foot Woman*, 1958

On Sweater Addiction, Going Cold Turkey:

I tried to keep away from these things. I tried, honestly, I tried. I hadn't had a stitch of them on for nearly a week. And then I couldn't take it anymore. I had to put it on or go out of my mind!

Glen (or was it Glenda?), played by Ed Wood, explaining his obsession with fluffy sweaters in *Glen or Glenda?*, 1952

On the Swinging Life:

Where sin begets sin. Nobody cares who does what to whom. Stripped of all inhibitions, everybody swings. No matter what your kick is, you name it, they've got it. They couldn't wait to get into the hotbed of pleasure. Charged-up, sex-crazed women, driven by bizarre desires. Choice women, from the fleshpots of the world, each with their own specialty . . . and you can have them all. Where violence begets violence. Where for just one night of twisted pleasures, men turn into beasts.

Announcer during a promo for *Where Sin Lives*, 1963

T

On Tabbies, Tough:

THE CATS ARE HUNGRY . . .
RUN FOR YOUR LIVES!
Alone, only a harmless pet.
One Thousand Strong, They Become a Man-Eating
Machine!

Ad for *The Night of a Thousand Cats*, 1972

On the Tabonga, You Know One When You See One:

Native woman: I just saw the Tabonga!
Witch doctor: Well, how do you know it was Tabonga?
Native woman: Because it looked like a tree and it had eyes and hands!

Natives forecasting doom in the radioactive-tree-gone-berserk horror film *From Hell It Came*, 1957

On Talks in the Ladies' Room, Ones We'd Like to Overhear:

While you were plugging your stepfather, your husband was plugging me – and he was *great*!

Kim Cattrall to Meg Tilly in the ladies' room during a dinner party in *Masquerade*, 1988

On Tearing Off Someone's Arm, Why Not to be Upset:

So what? He had *two*.

Explanation as to why he tore off a suspect's arm, given by cop and Harvard grad Carl Weathers in *Action Jackson*, 1988

On Teenage Girls, Difficult:

Hospital orderly: She was suffering from paranoia and hallucinations, induced by tranquillizers, cocaine, amphetamines, alcohol . . .
Mother (shrugging): She's always been difficult.

Bibi Besch as the mother of tramp-actress Pia Zadora in *The Lonely Lady*, 1983

On Teenagers, Clever:

Demonstrator: We want peace not police.
Girlfriend: Hey, that rhymes.

Teen longhairs in *Riot on Sunset Strip*, 1967

On Teen Dialogue, Great Moments in:

When I have a naughty dream at night she makes me feel like hanging myself.

Sandra Dee as Molly, talking about her repressive mother in *A Summer Place*, 1959

On Television Broadcasts, Ones You Never Hear in Real Life:

First man: This is KTTV Studios in Hollywood to Mount Wilson. We are being attacked by the Slime People. They have us walled in the city. If you have any information about this wall, please contact us immediately.

Second man: If anybody's listening, this is no joke. I'm a marine. I was fighting the Slime People and was knocked out. I guess they thought I was dead and left me there. The Slime People made a fog, and the fog turned to a wall. If anyone knows how to get through this thing, then I'm sure that there's a few other people just like us, that still have hope.

Broadcast from a deserted TV station in Los Angeles in *The Slime People*, 1962

On Television News, Typical:

The level of the mysterious radiation continues to increase steadily. So long as this situation remains, government spokesmen warn that dead bodies will continue to be transformed into the flesh-eating ghouls.

TV newsman giving the world the bad news in *Night of the Living Dead*, 1968

On Things We Hope We Never Hear on a Date:

If I didn't really work for the government, if I was just a guy who accidentally killed his parents, would you still love me?

Arsonist Anthony Perkins to schoolgirl Tuesday Weld in
Pretty Poison, 1968

On Things We Never Want to Hear:

The town is infested with man-eating cockroaches!
Repeat: man-eating cockroaches!

George Peppard calling Jan-Michael Vincent to tell him about
what the nuclear fallout has wrought in *Damnation Alley*,
1977

On Things You Don't Want to Hear Your Sexual Partner Saying:

Erogenous zones responding . . . sublingual glands
secreting.

Kristina Holland as a medical student recording her own
sexual responses in *Doctors' Wives*, 1970

On Things You Might Hear at 3 A.M. on New Year's Eve:

There is a herd of killer rabbits heading this way!

Panicky sheriff warning teenagers at the drive-in of
impending doom in *Night of the Lepus*, 1972

On Things You Should Never, Never Do:

Producer: Do you know what you've done? You've just
masturbated in front of all Paris!

Nijinsky: It wasn't me. It was the faun.

Alan Bates to George De La Pena playing the famed dancer Nijinsky, after the scandalous performance of 'Afternoon of a Faun' in *Nijinsky*, 1980

On Those Constantly Returning Volcanic Urges, Ageing Socialites and:

When that volcanic urge of yours comes back – and it will – you'll come to me!

Ageing socialite Genevieve Page, losing her young lover (James Franciscus in the title role) in *Youngblood Hawke*, 1964

On Those Crazy Scientists:

Man! The doc must have been brewing some of that Jekyll and Hyde joy juice in here.

Deputy inspecting the trashed lab after the two-headed transplant has escaped in *The Incredible Two-Headed Transplant*, 1971

On Those Ubiquitous Seth-ites:

Over there is the Temple of Seth. Two years ago they were just another snake cult. Now they're everywhere.

Conan the Barbarian, 1984

JOKES THAT FALL FLAT

A bad joke is truly a bad thing. Most bad jokes are happily forgotten – the teller quickly moves on to other jokes as he or she surveys the blank faces of an uncomprehending and hostile audience. But flat, stale jokes that are preserved on film are there forever, and remain to annoy or bore countless audiences in the future.

There are many purveyors of bad jokes in film, but the cinematic work in 1960s Dean Martin films perhaps stands out as the exemplar of awful taste in hilarity. One must realize that it takes a special something to produce jokes so awful they produce more than loud groans, an inverse talent happily denied most screenwriters. Here are some of the best of the worst jokes in movie history.

On Double Entendres, Pitiful:

Matt Helm (Dean Martin) to his buxom co-star: Oh, when you say you're a thirty-eight you ain't just kidding.

Linda: It's not a gun, Mr Helm. It's the new weapon they gave me, developed right here in our labs.

Matt: Developed pretty well, too!

Linda: May I point out –

Matt: You already do!

Linda: – that's why you're here. To become familiar with our latest equipment.

Matt: You're right. An agent should always keep *abreast* of the times!

The Ambushers, 1967

On Broads, Enlightening:

Matt: We have a long wait ahead of us so let's get comfortable.
Sheila: How comfortable?
Matt: It's broad daylight!
Sheila: What's the matter with a broad in daylight?

Dean Martin and Janice Rule in *The Ambushers*, 1967

On Congressmen, Typical:

Erin: Hi, I'm Erin Grant.
Congressman: Uh, I'm Congressman Dil . . . Dildo. Uh, Dilbeck.

Stripper Erin Grant (Demi Moore) meeting Congressman David Dilbeck (Burt Reynolds) on a yacht where she has come to do a command performance strip show in *Striptease*, 1996

On Haven't We Heard This One Before?:

Colleen Sutton: Nothing disgusts me. At the age of eleven I walked in on my father and the Shetland pony. Does that excite you?
Ford Fairlane: I don't know, I never met your father!

Andrew Dice Clay as Ford Fairlane, and Priscilla Presley in *The Adventures of Ford Fairlane*, 1990

On Puns, Pitiful:

Dean: 673 Wongs in the phone book.
Jerry: Hmm, that's a helluva lot of Wong numbers.

> Michael Kastorin and Scott Eddo in Bruce Willis's *Hudson Hawk*, 1991

On Time Travellers, Typical Complaints from:

I'm from another time, another place. I don't even know what you people have for lunch!

> Traveller from the future having a discussion with a twentieth-century woman in *Trancers*, 1985, starring Tim Thomerson and Helen Hunt

On the Tingler:

Ladies and Gentlemen, please do not panic, but scream. Scream for your lives! The Tingler is loose in *this* theatre, and if you don't scream, it may kill you!

> Vincent Price narration for *The Tingler*, 1959, in which the audience theatre seats started 'tingling' as though the deadly crab monster 'the Tingler' were loose in the theatre. The ads for this 'Percepto' technique claimed, 'You actually feel real physical sensations as you shiver to its flesh-crawling action!'

On Tiny Eyes, What They Mean:

From your tiny eyes, I can tell you won't be lazy in bed.

Sexpot Sharla Cheung Man in *Holy Weapon*, 1993

On Tough Guys, Really Modest:

Delilah: But you might have been hurt!
Samson: It was nothing. It was only a *young* lion.

Hedy Lamarr and Victor Mature in the title roles, after Samson wrestles a lion to death with his hands in *Samson and Delilah*, 1949

On Tough Guys, Tough-to-Follow Orders for:

Beat him out of recognizable shape!

English subtitle in Jackie Chan's kung fu classic *Police Story II*, 1988

On Tough Talk, Painful:

Dr Elizabeth Clay: I'll give you a local.
Dalton: No, thank you.
Dr Elizabeth Clay: Do you enjoy pain?
Dalton: Pain don't hurt.

Conversation between astoundingly beautiful emergency room doctor (Kelly Lynch) and incredibly cool new bar bouncer in town (Patrick Swayze), while she's stitching up his knife wound in *Road House*, 1989

On Tourist Traps, Literal:

Crazed townsperson (looking at the corpse of a tourist who was just pushed down a hill in a barrel with sharp nails hammered into it):
Doggone! If this ain't the best centennial anybody ever had!

Two Thousand Maniacs, 1965

On Translation, Great Primate Moments in:

Amy the Talking Gorilla (pointing): Mother!
Peter: Mother?
Amy the Talking Gorilla: Ooh, ooh!
Peter: Oh, I see. *Africa* is your mother!

Amy the Talking Gorilla having a philosophical discussion with Dr Peter Elliott (Dylan Walsh) at the end of *Congo*, 1995

On Trash, Trash, Trash:

I know what ya think, that I'm trashy like my ma! . . . Trash, trash, trash, trash, *trash*!

Half-breed Indian gal Jennifer Jones in *Duel in the Sun*, 1946

On Trees, Hard to Imagine:

Nurse: How did that tree get here?
Scientist: In plain English, it walked here.
Nurse: It's hard to imagine carnivorous trees that move on their own roots.
Scientist: Not carnivorous: omnivorous. All-devouring. He'll eat anything – even other trees.

Mamie Van Doren and Walter Sande having a scientific discussion in *The Navy vs. the Night Monsters*, 1966

On Trick Questions, Bizarre:

Abby: Have you ever had the bad mumps?
Postman: Never had the bad mumps.
Abby: Syphilis? Nothin' like that?
Postman: [shakes head]
Abby: So, as far as you know, you have good semen?
Postman: Is that a trick question?

Young post-holocaust frontier woman, Abby (Olivia Williams), looking for a father for her wished-for child and hoping she's found him in the visiting mailman (Kevin Costner) in *The Postman*, 1997

On Tricky Words Men of Medical Science Use:

Psychiatrist: You're referring to the suicide of the transvestite?
Policeman: If that's the word you men of medical science use for a man who wears women's clothing, yes.

Timothy Farrell as the doctor and Lyle Talbot as the cop in *Glen or Glenda?*, 1952

On Turtles, Why They Step on People:

Gamera doesn't mean to step on people. He's just lonely. Even turtles get lonely sometimes.

Child defending a giant turtle who is terrorizing Tokyo in *Gamera, the Invincible*, 1965

On Twin Peaks, Co-starring:

What a Guy! What a Gal! What a Pair!

Ad for *Stroker Ace*, 1983, starring the well-endowed Loni Anderson and Burt Reynolds

On Two-Headed Men, Possible Benefits of:

Girlfriend, looking at her now two-headed boyfriend's crotch: Honey, I was wondering . . . um . . . do you have two of anything else?

Chelsea Brown to two-headed Rosey Grier/Ray Milland man in *The Thing with Two Heads*, 1972

On Two-Headed Monsters:

These things have a way of attracting attention, you know.

Concerned scientist to his wife after the two-headed-man-monster escapes from his lab in *The Manster*, 1959

On Tycoons Who Won't End Up on the Cover of <u>Time</u>:

If only your father could see you now: the world's richest man, crazy like a fox, wearing a dress, with parrot shit on his shoulders.

Alcoholic wife (Jane Lapotaire) to sad but wacky and rich Gene Hackman in *Eureka*, 1981

u

On Understatements, Great Moments in:

What a crazy day! The first time I've seen you in three years and we're buried alive!

A woman making conversation with an old boyfriend in *Cave-In!*, 1983

On Understatements, Medical:

You're sure it isn't measles?

Lee Strasberg to famous doctor Richard Harris, who has trapped a demented terrorist afflicted with a horrible plague virus in *The Cassandra Crossing*, 1976

On Understatements of the Century, Titanic:

This is bad.

Leonardo DiCaprio in *Titanic*, 1997, as the ship hits the giant iceberg

On Untranslatable Unpronounceable Names:

Although his name is untranslatable to any known Earth language, it would sound something like . . . Zontar!

NASA scientist explaining an alien invader in *Zontar, the Thing from Venus*, 1968

V

On Vampires, Artificial:

We're vampires, all right, but only in a synthetic sense.

Hip (and hippie) vampiress in *The Wild Wild World of Batwoman (She Was a Happy Vampire)*, a.k.a. *She Was a Hippy* [sic] *Vampire*, 1966

On Vampires of Colour, Proclivities of:

African vampires don't go for Chinese women.

Jackie Chan's *Armour of God II: Operation Candor*, 1991

On Venusians, Typically Uncooperative:

I think you're wondering how you might get us to reveal our knowledge of interplanetary travel. And how you might force that information from us. Others of you are estimating the heights to which you might rise if you could personally arrange for our cooperation in space travel techniques. Well, forget it.

The Venusian (Helmut Dantine) dashing all our hopes in *Stranger from Venus*, 1954

On Viewing a Decapitated Head, Great Insights About:

Maybe his head just got loose and *fell* off!

> Explanation given by detective (David Carradine) as to how a window washer was decapitated in *Q*, 1982

On Vultan, Those Crazy Habits of:

Mongo security man: The Earth people have been captured by hawkmen and taken to the sky city of King Vultan.

Ming: Where no doubt Vultan will compel the Earth girl to marry him. It is a habit of his.

Flash Gordon, 1938

On Wabbits, Vewy Scawy:

The Terror of the Monster Rabbits – Out to Destroy Everything in their Path . . . They Multiply, They Weigh 150 Pounds, They're Four Feet Tall – and They Kill . . . Dynamite Won't Stop the Hopping of These Giants.

Ad for *Night of the Lepus*, 1972

On Warnings, Kind of Confusing:

Beware! Beware! Beware of the big green dragon that sits on your doorstep! He eats little boys! Puppy dog tails! Big fat snails! Beware! Take care! Beware!

Narrator 2 (Bela Lugosi) describing a scene of buffalo herds and atom bombs in *Glen or Glenda?*, 1953

On Welcomes, Ones That Don't Sound All That Great:

You will be welcome in Zukuru! The headman's locust bean cakes – they'll be your locust bean cakes! His fermented buffalo milk will be your fermented buffalo milk.

Sheena (Tanya Roberts) declaring her undying love for Ted Wass in *Sheena*, 1984

On Western Clichés, Clichéd:

That's a lot of man you're carrying in those boots, stranger.

John Carradine to new cowpoke in town, Johnny (Sterling Hayden), in *Johnny Guitar*, 1954

On What Doctors Say to Patients Who Have Turned into Brain-Eating Monsters:

It looks like you're experiencing some complications.

Doctor to patient who is turning into a brain-eating monster after having received some experimental youth-serum injections in *Rejuvenatrix*, 1988

On What Life Really Is, World-Weary Thoughts About:

Nancy: We're all spoiled for choice, aren't we, darling? I knew after the first three days and nights that I'd blown it. I married for love instead of money. I came home and I found him sleeping in my garter belt. So, I left him and married a Mexican who owned an ocean liner and two hundred acres of Acapulco, and after about a week I knew that I'd really blown it. Here I am in the bathroom, utterly pissed, alone on my birthday, without love, without money, asking myself, 'What else is there?'
Claire: Ambition and a half-hour of prime-time TV.

Jodie Foster (Nancy) complaining and Ellen Barkin (Claire) answering in *Siesta*, 1987

On What Not to Pack for Your Honeymoon:

A corpse has no place on a honeymoon.

Conversation in *Dead Men Tell*, 1941

On What People Who Give Names to Their Breasts Say:

Wife, showing one of her breasts to her husband: Like it? Want to kiss it? Its name is Jasmine. But I can't let you – because Cyclamen will get jealous.

Soon-to-be-dead wife Nathalie Delon to husband and soon-to-be-murderer Richard Burton in *Bluebeard*, 1972

On What They Talk About in Space:

First astronaut: Why, it's a woman!
Second astronaut: You can say that again – with all the necessary ingredients!

Two astonished astronauts meeting a woman on the thirteenth moon of Jupiter in *Fire Maidens of Outer Space*, 1955

On What to Say After Your Lunch Partner's Face Has Been Eaten by Slugs:

Businesswoman: God! You never saw anything like what happened in that restaurant.
Businessman: Oh, put it out of your mind, Sue!
Businesswoman: How? His whole face was . . .

Mayor: Uh, can I freshen your drinks?
Businesswoman: I sure hope things like that don't happen
around here again!

Man and woman, who had been trying to consummate a
business deal with the slug's lunch, having a conversation
with the town's mayor in *Slugs*, 1988

On What to Say to an Alien:

Alien: It should interest you to know that I have visited
hundreds of other worlds and your Earth seems most
suitable.
Submarine commander: Swell!

Bug-eyed alien and Earth fellow having a conversation in *The
Atomic Submarine*, 1959

On What to Say to Giant Evil Cucumbers:

I hate your living guts! You're ugly! You think you're going
to make a slave of the world. Go on. Try your intellect on
me!

Scientist's wife (Beverly Garland) confronting the giant
cucumber that is trying to take over Earth in *It Conquered
the World*, 1956

On What to Say to Giant Man-Killing Apes:

I'm a Libra. What sign are you? No wait, don't tell me. I
bet you're an Aries, aren't you?

Jessica Lange as Dwan, the lady in distress, to Kong in *King
Kong*, 1976

On What to Say to a Killer Whale:

I'd tell him I didn't mean to kill his wife. I'd tell him I was
sorry . . .

> Sea captain Richard Harris explaining what he'd say to the
> killer Orca whale he is hunting in *Orca*, 1977

On What to Say to Lovely Russian Secret Agents:

I always think of you as two girls: Anna, the lovely kid I
thought was a refugee, and Olga, a Soviet Tootsie Roll that
made a chump out of me.

> All-American pilot John Wayne, to his love, the Russian
> double agent Janet Leigh, in *Jet Pilot*, 1957

On What to Say to Psycho Commanders Before They Detonate Nuclear Warheads:

You need to get some sleep!

> Navy SEAL to his psychotic commander, who is about to
> detonate a nuclear warhead underwater that will kill them all
> in *The Abyss*, 1989

On What to Say to Slow-Moving Women:

You're moving like a deeply offended Tibetan yak!

> Crazed movie director Peter Finch, to his new protégée Kim
> Novak in *The Legend of Lylah Clare*, 1968

On What to Say to Smiling Bad Guys:

It would be less repugnant to be strangled by a thousand serpents than to have to endure your smile.

Princess Mila (Lisa Foster) to the evil villain in *The Blade Master*, 1984

On What to Say to a Woman on a Deserted Isle:

If the gods had meant me for another, then why, why, did they send you? Marry me at once – or leave my island!

South Seas hunk (Dayton Ka'ne) to his deserted island find Mia Farrow in *Hurricane*, 1979

On What to Say to Your Other Head:

Moron: Who are you?
Maniac: I'm your brother.
Moron: I don't have a brother.
Maniac: You do now.
Moron: My neck hurts.
Maniac: Our neck hurts, stupid!

The newly transplanted heads having one of their first discussions in *The Incredible Two-Headed Transplant*, 1971

ED WOOD: THE KING OF THE STUPID MOVIE LINE

The lover of stupid movie lines finds a gold mine in the films of producer/writer/director/actor Ed Wood, who also cheerfully delivers incomprehensible plots, wooden acting, bizarre continuity, and horrifyingly bad scenery. His magnum opus, *Plan 9 from Outer Space*, has been consistently voted the worst movie of all time, but other films of his are just as bad. Wood had a tragic life – among other things he was a cross-dresser (he wore pink knickers underneath his Marine uniform during World War II) before such behaviour became yawningly clichéd, and he suffered during the 1950s and 1960s as a misunderstood, perversely bad genius . . . if genius is the word.

Today, of course, it is all different, and Wood has achieved in death an odd sort of cinematic success that was denied him in life. His film career was brought to the silver screen in an eponymous movie starring Johnny Depp, and today he has a legion of fans who can happily repeat verbatim the many screenplay gaffes that truly make him the Dan Quayle or Yogi Berra of incomprehensibly odd or bizarre (stupid doesn't seem to be quite the right word) movie lines.

On Great Thoughts of Modern Man:

Modern man is a hardworking human.

Psychiatrist (Timothy Farrell) in *Glen or Glenda?*, 1952

On Comebacks to Aliens, Great Moments in:

Colonel Edwards: Why is it so important that you want to contact the governments of our Earth?

Eros the Alien: Because of death. *Because all of you of Earth are idiots!*

Fighter pilot: Now, you just hold on, buster!

Tom Keene (the colonel), Dudley Manlove (the alien), and Gregory Walcott (the pilot), in *Plan 9 from Outer Space*, 1959

On Dialogues with Aliens, Great Moments in:

Eros the Alien: Your scientists stumbled upon the atom bomb – split the atom! Then the hydrogen bomb, where you actually explode the air itself. Now you bring the total destruction of the entire universe, served by our sun. The only explosion left is the solaronite.

Fighter pilot: So what if we do develop this solaronite bomb – we'd be even a stronger nation than now!

Eros the Alien: Stronger? You see! You see! Your stupid minds! Stupid! Stupid!

Fighter pilot: That's all I'm taking from you! [He punches the alien.]

Dudley Manlove (the alien) and Gregory Walcott (the pilot), in *Plan 9 from Outer Space*, 1959

On Baldness, Interesting Thoughts About:

Men's hats are so tight they cut off the blood flow to the head, thus cutting off the growth of hair. Seven out of ten men wear hats, so the advertisements say. Seven out of ten men are bald! But what about the ladies? Yes, modern woman is a hardworking individual also. But when modern woman's day of work is done, that which is designed for her home comfort, is comfort. Hats that give no obstruction to the blood flow. Hats that do not crush the hair. Interesting thought, isn't it?

Psychiatrist (Timothy Farrell) in *Glen or Glenda?*, 1952

On Things You Never Learned at the Police Academy:

Monsters, space people, mad doctors. They didn't teach me about such things at the police academy.

Officer Kelton (Paul Marco) complaining in *Night of the Ghouls*, 1959

On Fantastic Stories, Fantastic!:

Colonel: This is the most fantastic story I've ever heard!
Pilot: And every word of it's true, too.
Colonel: That's the fantastic part of it!

Plan 9 from Outer Space, 1959

On What to Say When You're Making Love to Another Man on Your Dead Husband's Grave:

I've never kept anything from him. He'd like to know.

> Beautiful widow explaining her actions in *Cemetery Man*, 1995

On What to Say When You See a Burning Lake with Horrible Monsters Swimming Around:

I don't like the look of this lake, sir.

> Crewman expressing some doubts about the burning lake filled with horrible monsters in *The Land That Time Forgot*, 1975

On What to Say When You See a Giant Man-Eating Bird:

Pilot 1: I've seen some mighty big chicken hawks back on the farm, but this one takes the cake.
Pilot 2: Honest to Pete, I'll never call my mother-in-law an old crow again!

> Pilots discussing the giant man-eating bird in *The Giant Claw*, 1957

On What to Say When You See a Giant Slime Mould:

What you are looking at is no ordinary plant!

Japanese scientist explaining a horrendous sight in the slime-mould thriller *Godzilla vs. Biollante*, 1989

On What to Say When You See a Ten-foot Chicken:

Where the hell did you get these goddamned chickens?

Morgan (Marjoe Gortner) to the farm wife, after he has been attacked by a ten-foot-tall chicken in the barn, in *Food of the Gods*, 1976

On What to Say When You've Been Rejected:

I'm gonna go see if I can scare up a gang bang.

Laraine Newman after unsuccessfully trying to seduce John Travolta in *Perfect*, 1985

On What Town Mayors Worry About:

How are we going to fight them? They're all dead!

Worried town mayor in *Return of the Blind Dead*, 1972

On Women, Gooselike:

They are so horny . . . sometimes at night you can hear them honking.

Sid Haig to Jerry Frank about the female cons in women-behind-bars film *The Big Doll House*, 1971

On Women, Illogical Points About:

Women! With 'em, without 'em, who could live?

Christopher Walken, fed up with nympho bank worker Anne Heche in *Wild Side*, 1995

On Women, Probably Popular with the Opposite Sex:

She is a pulverizing crucible of fulfilment.

Narrator in *Beneath the Valley of the Ultra-Vixens*, 1979, a Russ Meyer film

On Women, Typical 1950s Dialogue from:

Oh, Bob, honey, you're just so strong and big and brave. I don't know what I'd do without you.

Bob's girlfriend before she and Bob (Mike Connors) are captured by the three bad Nardo girls in *Swamp Women*, 1955

On Women, What Men Really Want from:

Desert horseman: Your beauty and charms are beyond compare. But can you weave a saddle blanket from the wool of a Nubian goat? Or plait a horsehair rope?

Sultan's daughter: No! No! Neither will I chew tanned horsehide until it becomes soft and pliable for the shoes of a desert scavenger!

Horseman: Well, then, high and mighty princess, of what earthly use are you to a man?

Jeff Chandler and Maureen O'Hara in *Flame of Araby*, 1951

On Work Problems, Overreactions to:

Other men have disappointments, but they don't become animals!

Long-suffering wife Barbara Rush to husband Cameron Mitchell when he rapes his next-door neighbour after he doesn't get promoted in *No Down Payment*, 1957

On Wrath, Beautiful Moments:

Bortai (trying to kill him): For me, there is no peace while you live, Mongol!

Genghis Khan: You're beautiful in your wrath!

John Wayne and Susan Hayward in *The Conqueror*, 1956

On You Think You've Got Problems?:

Nellie: I've got a husband who's drunk all the time and a growing girl dressing and undressing in front of him and him staring at her all the time and staring at her and thinking. And staring . . .
Connie: Oh, Nellie! We all have our problems!

Nellie, the mother of a girl who's just been raped by her father, trying to talk to her employer Connie (Lana Turner), in *Peyton Place*, 1957

On Yiddish Sayings, Kind of Schmeared:

Terrible day! Oy vay, what a day! What a schmear!

Whitley Strieber (Christopher Walken), sensitive New York writer, mis-saying the Yiddish 'Oy vay iz meer', in *Communion*, 1989

Z

On the Zombie Stomp, Great Moments with:

Oh, everybody do the zombie stomp!
Doo-doo-doo-doop.
Just land your foot down with an awful bump!
Doo-doo-doo-doop.
Baby, baby, don't you care?
Something here looking kinda weird.
Honey, I'm no Frankenstein.
Oh yeah, baby, really I feel fine.

> 'The Zombie Stomp', sung by the Del-Aires in *The Horror of Party Beach*, 1964

On Zombies, Clever:

Those dead people sure are smart!

> Man trying to escape from zombies, when he discovers that the zombies have taken the distributor cap out of the escape vehicle in *Dead Pit*, 1989

Now you can order superb titles directly from Michael O'Mara Books.

(tick boxes below)

The One Hundred Stupidest Things Ever Done	Ross & Kathryn Petras	£3.99	☐
The Stupidest Things Ever Said	Ross & Kathryn Petras	£3.99	☐
Stupid Sex	Ross & Kathryn Petras	£3.99	☐
Stupid Things Men Do		£3.99	☐
The World's Stupidest Laws		£3.99	☐
The World's Stupidest Signs		£3.99	☐
The Little Book of Farting	Alec Bromcie	£1.99	☐
The Complete Book of Farting	Alec Bromcie	£4.99	☐

Sub total _____

Please allow for postage and packing:
UK: free delivery
Europe: add 20% of retail price
Rest of World: add 30% of retail price

Total _____

To order any of the above or any other Michael O'Mara titles, please call our credit card orderline or fill in this coupon and post / fax to:

Michael O'Mara Books, 250 Western Avenue, London W3 6EE, UK

Telephone 020 8324 5652   Facsimile 020 8324 5678

☐ I enclose a UK bank cheque made payable to MOM Bookshop Ltd for £ _____

☐ Please charge £ _____ to my Access/Visa/Delta/Switch

Card No. ☐☐☐☐☐☐☐☐☐☐☐☐☐☐☐☐☐☐☐☐

Expiry Date: ☐☐ / ☐☐   Switch Issue No. ☐☐

NAME (Block Letters please): _____

ADDRESS: _____

_____

POSTCODE: _____   TELEPHONE: _____

SIGNATURE: _____